The Making of Faith

By

Victoria Baker

THE MAKING OF FAITH

Written & Photographed
by Victoria Baker

Library of Congress Control Number:
2015901082
Baker, Victoria 1959-
The Making of Faith/Victoria Baker
Published by Victoria Baker
Red Bank, NJ USA

ISBN: 978-0692305386 (paperback)
ISBN: 0692305386 (eBook)

DEDICATION

To the One who loves me for me. Thank you Father,
thank you Jesus, thank you Spirit of Life.
With gratitude and love for all that you have been,
who you are in this moment, who you will always be.
You have made me for You, for Love.

All Knowing Creator God, you are
amazing, magnificent, and gentle,
and I thank you and love you.

CONTENTS

FOREWORD

"The Making of Faith" has been in my friend Vicky's heart for many years, and has brought the two of us together countless times. When Vicky and her boys first came to our church, I invited her out for coffee. We first connected by sharing highlights about our families and careers before moving onto more personal stories. During our second time together, Vicky mentioned her plan to write a book someday, and I somehow volunteered to help her by proofreading it. That very afternoon, Vicky sent the first installment of "The Making of Faith"! As the weeks passed, the continuous stream of stories that Vicky shared captivated me.

Working with Vicky on this book provided many opportunities that enriched my own relationship with God. It increased my own faith, and made me more aware of God's presence in my life: His love, His blessings, His peace. I hope everyone who reads this book is similarly rewarded.

Thank you, Vicky, for the joy and privilege of sharing four years of coffee, and including me in your journey of faith.

Sarah Lawser

THE FALL
2005

Broken ~ My Story

Everyone faces challenges, and my husband Bud and I were no exception. Throughout our 23-year marriage, we dealt with job loss, years of infertility, illness, our sons' developmental delays and medical issues, and the responsibility for elderly relatives in failing health. There was a lot to deal with, but we had each other.

Our son Ian was diagnosed with autism, and we planned to move to a town that could provide special resources and support. In the months before our move, Bud seemed cold, almost indifferent to me. It puzzled me, but he insisted all was well, and we made the move. All was well, until suddenly it wasn't.

With no warning, my husband wanted to start a new life without me. He stuffed his clothes into a hefty bag, left our home, and ended our marriage. I was stunned, then broken.

Eerily enough, the very day before Bud left, I'd had an odd foreboding during my prayer time. *"I will always be with you,"* God's words resonated deep in my spirit. *Oh, I don't like the sound of this at all,* was my return. *"You will never walk alone,"* *Oh boy, I thought to myself, this can't be good. What could He mean? What do you mean Lord?*

After Bud left, I felt abandoned and completely alone, but at least intellectually, I remembered God's promise to never leave me. Those words hovered when I felt like a bullet had exploded inside of me. I couldn't catch my breath; the emotional pain was truly physical.

Life unraveled, and it seemed quite possible for the earth to crack open and swallow me up, please. I hated everything about that uncomfortable, uncertain road.

I've come a long way since those dark days. Prayer has been a means of creating and sustaining a special connection to the Lord. In learning to surrender, trust, believe, and have faith, our lives were transformed; we were made new.

His Loving Presence was also revealed in the sudden arrival of friends, therapists, and advocates who arrived in our life at just the right time, sometimes at our very doorstep.

I learned that an attitude of thankfulness, and the willingness to forgive, could move us through pain and grief into peace and happiness.

My sons and I are proof that God truly cares; He has touched our lives with His Divine Love.   This journey has transformed us.   We've evolved from a victim mentality to becoming go-getters, broken to whole, sad to joyful, helpless to empowered.   God *never* breaks His promises.   He is always with us, and He never leaves us the same.   *Thank you Father.*

May our experiences help reveal God's promises to everyone who reads this book.

To The Left

We didn't know our neighbor Mrs. Parker well at all. We'd hardly spoken since our arrival nine months before, mostly just waving and smiling across the lawns. A few weeks after Bud had left, I received a knock on the door. When I opened the door, her sweet face was inquisitive.

Surprisingly, she simply announced, "In my spirit when I was praying, the Lord told me to pray for the people to the left of me, and that would be you." *Oh, You are good Lord.* Back then it didn't take much for my waterworks to start. Her arrival triggered them once again.

I invited her in, we embraced and prayed. I will always be grateful for that day. For a good number of months afterward, Mrs. Parker stopped by to see if I was okay. I wasn't, but I knew someday I would be. God was always with us before, why not now?

Mrs. Parker would bring bible videos and toys for the kids. She lovingly spoke to the boys, and comforted me. During one of her visits, I shared that God had put it in my heart to write a book. I asked Mrs. Parker if we could pray about what God wanted me to do next. I shared how the Lord had always been faithful in so many challenges in our lives. How should I begin this book? How could I make it authentic for believers, and real for those who had never heard of this Jesus, my Savior? Brainstorming, however little my brain could handle then, we exchanged ideas.

What if each story of God's goodness connected with verses from the bible? What if His word was the breath that we all needed to continue when life got hard, or when it was just fabulous?

What if I could show that scripture was not just ancient words written thousands of years ago? That His words are alive and full of Love today, speaking to us in our circumstances? Mrs. Parker's words of wisdom were, "Keep it brief and loving." I let her advice and God's calling many years ago settle into my being.

"Keep this Book of the Law always on your lips; meditate on it day and night,
so that you may be careful to do everything written in it.
Then you will be prosperous and successful."
- Joshua 1:8 (NIV)* [1]

Time passed as it always does. Mrs. Parker decided it was time to move and scale down from the home her children were raised in, so up went the for sale sign. As she rummaged through her belongings she found a treasure. One day, speakers and stereo in tow, she appeared at the door again. A dated record and cassette player arrived in our care, musty and dusty. They were now ours but I would not use them for some time. Music makes me feel, and I didn't want to feel anything.

While I knew to pray, I would soon learn that *praising* our Creator through another storm of my life would turn everything around for our good, so amazing.

"Therefore, since we have a great high priest who has ascended into heaven,
Jesus the Son of God, let us hold firmly to the faith
we profess. For we do not have a high priest who is unable
to empathize with our weaknesses,
but we have one who has been tempted in every way,
just as we are—yet he did not sin.

Let us then approach God's throne of grace
with confidence, so that we may receive mercy
and find grace to help us in our time of need."
- Hebrews 4:14-16 (NIV")

I found verses in the bible that were promises for us, and recited them out loud throughout the house before I started my day, before the calls and emails, meetings, insurance appeals, etc.! Holding onto those verses, I believed that God loved Ian, Danny and me, no matter what.

But I didn't feel peace automatically, no way. I realized I struggled more than necessary. My way of trying to control and handle everything on my own was not God's way.

On my knees, praying, talking, singing, going to His throne of Grace, I praised God for His mercy and His goodness. I believed in healing, in someone who could make a way for Ian's education, his healing. I believed Danny and Ian would be gifts to many, that both their hearts would survive their father's absence and thrive. It was not wishful thinking. God's word says that we are children of the Most High God, and I believed it by faith, not by what was in front of me each day. When I believed it the day passed by easy, but when I took over, what could go wrong, well, you know. *Thank you Lord for answered prayers.*

"So we fix our eyes not on what is seen,
but on what is unseen,
since what is seen is temporary,

but what is unseen is eternal."
– 2 Corinthians 4:18 (NIV)*

Before I put my feet on the floor to this day, I talk to the Father, Jesus, and Holy Spirit. Asking for strength for the day, I begin, *Thank you Father for this new day, the gift of life, the breath of life, the promise of life with You.* I was sure I didn't have enough faith in myself, so I left it all up to Him. I had to.

Within a year of that special day God sent Mrs. Parker to our doorstep, she had sold her home for a new life in a new town.

Ten years later, the music plays on from that ol' stereo with the likes of Carly Simon, Carole King, and even Pink Floyd. Danny, so struck with the clear sounds of the stereo, officially began his own record collection. *God does make things new, again and again,* I thought to myself as Danny listened to *"The Dark Side of the Moon."* I also laughed inside wondering what Mrs. Parker would think about Pink Floyd.

As I write, the world is in chaos. Wars, terrorists, global warming, unemployment, polarizing issues, gun violence, increased autism and Alzheimer's, and racism headline our daily news. And yet I think of the One who gives us our daily bread, His heart, our lives. Isn't that enough? I know I need to surrender each day to His Love, and I *know* His Word.

I wonder about those who are so far from God for whatever reason, perhaps they have never been introduced, or perhaps they think they are not worthy of a Love like that?

I am changed. I know God has carried us through our heartaches. This cannot just be our story alone.

We Are Here For You

My parents had gone on vacation the day Bud left me. I couldn't bear to phone them while they were away from home. I did call a few dear friends who rallied around me, but no one was there to hug me. By the week's end, I found the strength to call my parents and tell them the news.

A few days passed. Returning from errands before picking up the kids at school, I found a huge, beautiful bouquet of flowers at my front door. I opened the card before I gathered them in my arms. Five little words scrolled through the big, white spaces of the card. In their own brokenness my parents wrote: "We are here for you." I carried the flowers inside.

God's whisper, "*I will always be with you. You will never walk alone*" kept me going.

> *"No one will be able to stand against you all the days of your life.*
> *As I was with Moses, so I will be with you;*
> *I will never leave you nor forsake you."*
> *- Joshua 1:5 (NIV)*

So many friends have lost mother or father over the years. I am blessed to have them both, happy and healthy. The kids are too. That spring day, I pulled myself together and retrieved the kids. Grateful then and now, God continues to bless us with my parents. Our relationship and sharing is more open, and the kids are much closer to their grandparents than ever before.

I think of the sweet flowers I couldn't enjoy on that spring day but they are with me now. They are reminiscent of my mother's perfume that lingers long after she visits. I can't tell you how many blessings have been showered over Danny, Ian and me since those early days of loss. They are too many to count. I do know His love is from day to day, from everlasting to everlasting. I am grateful for the sweet aroma of Jesus every day . . .

> *"But thanks be to God, who always leads us*
> *as captives in Christ's triumphal procession*
> *and uses us to spread the aroma of the knowledge of him everywhere."*
> *- 2 Corinthians 2:14 (NIV)*

Rainbows

Coming home from Ian's language therapy the day before the first anniversary of 9/11, we saw a rainbow stretched across the sky.

Much later on July 31ˢᵗ, 2004, I packed the kids up and took them to my parents. We were moving from a home and neighbors we loved and still do. We were moving to a better place for the kids, their future and education. It was hot and steamy, with on and off showers throughout the day, the kind of day you wish for a good snowstorm because of the heat.

We neared the exit from the highway, one that would signal we're almost home, and saw the rainbow. It was breathtaking. The kids were thrilled. When I see rainbows like this or incredible rays of sun, I always whisper, *Thank you Lord, I see you too.*

A week after my husband left, I was traveling down a local highway heading toward home. The early days were filled with sobbing, something I called "the crying hours." I would cry during school hours, and pull myself together to greet the boys. This day, Bud was spending time with the kids and I was giving them the space to do so. I had left Barnes & Noble feeling lost in a world full of books.

On the highway, to my left, I saw this magnificent rainbow. I felt God's enormous love for me. It quieted my heart. And right then, I knew everything would be alright. It may not be next month or even next year. But I knew someday I would find peace.

As I pulled into our driveway, huge drops of rain poured down. The bow appeared before the rain. This promise of His love is for all of us.

> *"And God said, "This is the sign of the covenant I am making*
> *between me and you and every living creature with you,*
> *a covenant for all generations to come:*
> *I have set my rainbow in the clouds,*
> *and it will be the sign of the covenant*
> *between me and the earth.*
> *Whenever I bring clouds over the earth*
> *and the rainbow appears in the clouds,*
> *I will remember my covenant*
> *between me and you and all living creatures of every kind.*
> *Never again will the waters become a flood to destroy all life."*
> *- Genesis 9: 12-15 (NIV²)*

The Whisper

I was desperate to be still. My mind was racing. I tend to project ahead, too far ahead. That's not a good thing at a time of loss. Losing my best friend just couldn't be real. I was living someone else's life. He couldn't be doing this to me. I felt erased. As the world went on about its business, I was trying to find a way to hang on.

He had the kids this particular Saturday. It was a beautiful, sunny day. I had no joy. Would he take care of them? Pay attention to them? Bring them home to me? These thoughts swirled through my head.

I had more than my share of chores raising the kids on my own. But I knew special time with Jesus was what I needed. After all, oversharing with everyone I met wasn't bringing me any comfort. From their gaping mouths, I could tell they regretted asking "How are you?" *Oh please help me find my mind!*

Roman Catholic churches usually keep communion hosts on the altar. Through the difficult times, I would kneel before the tabernacle and pray to Jesus. I always heard His voice. There, I was able to quiet my spinning thoughts and listen.

Outside, kids rode bikes and cars raced past: summer sounds. Inside however, church was empty, quiet, and mine. Jesus was waiting and I, searching. I knelt and pleaded. *Lord, where are you? Why can't I feel you? Why are you allowing this to happen to me?*

Haven't I loved you all my life? What have I done? I am so alone. This is not the place in my life where I should be. Why can't I find you? Stifling my sobs as if anyone was there, I heard, *"I am a whisper away."*

Feeling quite unlovely, I slid into the pew. I needed God's word. So I opened the bible readings for the week. The next day's reading was about Elijah the prophet. This is what was written:

"The LORD said, "Go out and stand on
the mountain in the presence of the
LORD, for the LORD is about to pass by.
Then a great and powerful wind tore the mountains
apart and shattered the rocks before the LORD,
but the LORD was not in the wind.
After the wind there was an earthquake,
but the LORD was not in the earthquake.

After the earthquake came a fire,
but the LORD was not in the fire.
And after the fire came a gentle whisper.
When Elijah heard it, he pulled his cloak over
his face and went out and stood at the mouth
of the cave. Then a voice said to him,
"What are you doing here, Elijah?"
- I Kings 19:11-14 (NIV®)

I felt Him so near in His whisper. With all the crazy things happening in the world, He remembered me - here in this tiny church located in the middle of town. *You are here with me. You have not forgotten me, forgive me Lord for doubting,* I said.

Aloud, I spoke, *You are so good to me Lord. Thank you, thank you, thank you.* Grateful tears mixed with joyful energy which became praise. *So awesome, so wonderful, so incredible are You, King of Kings and Lord of Lords. My Lord and my God,* I prayed.

"Though you have not seen him, you love him;
and even though you do not see him now,
you believe in him and are filled with an
inexpressible and glorious joy,"
- 1 Peter 1:8 (NIV®)

Treasures

Relatives outside your immediate family notice your life circumstances in a more astute way. One day an aunt reflected on the many struggles Bud and I had endured. After 13 years of marriage, Ian was born. Happily, Danny soon followed.

She commented that those little boys were my treasures. She went on to say, they always would be. Perhaps my aunt felt the connection to this beautiful passage found in the Gospel of Luke.

"For where your treasure is,
there your heart will be also."
– Luke 12:34 (NIV")

Thank you Spirit of Life. Wherever they walk in life, they will be my heart. Thank you Jesus for the priceless gifts of Ian, Danny, and Aunt Carole's wisdom.

Here I Am

During that initial season of loss, I often returned to church to pray for strength. I say initial because there are different levels of grief in a divorce. The world pretty much expects you to get on with life once some time has passed. But the separation from someone you've loved for so long comes with grief, shock and emotional trauma. It's a death. But the world doesn't acknowledge it as such. People have offered words. *"It's for the best." "It was a mistake." "The marriage was never what it should have been."* These words were not comforting after a lifetime together, and two kids later.

When there was true love in a marriage, its end is death. This was the death of trust, love and companionship. I did cling to God's Word, searching for His comfort, strength, and answers.

One summer afternoon when Bud took the kids for the day, I forged off to church. It is amazing how empty church is on an early Saturday afternoon. Still reeling from the shock, I sat in silence. I spoke to God in my heart, turning once again to confide in a dear friend. This was different. This was my Father, the One in heaven. My sarcastic self thought, *I need You here right now, don't you know?* There, I let myself cry. Being strong for the kids took everything. Writing this passage June of 2006, I think, of course He knew.

Another gorgeous, beautiful summer day, and there I was crying an ocean. Trying to make sense of it all wasn't working. Over the years, when I wanted to give thanks or pray for someone but words or prayers were not in my reach, I sang to God. One of my favorites has always been *"I The Lord of Sea and Sky,"* which is a song also known as *"Here I Am."*[1]

When I hear or sing that song, I feel so moved by His spirit. There is a divine connection. That Saturday, when my loss was so great, I grabbed the music book and searched. As I sang, there was a big cloud passing over. It quickly grew dark as I knelt.

My voice was not strong but I was able to manage. The end of the first stanza:

> *"I, who made the stars of night, I will make their darkness bright.*
> *Who will bear my light to them? Whom shall I send?*
> *Here I am, Lord. Is it I, Lord?"*

> *"I have heard you calling in the night. I will go,*
> *Lord, if you lead me. I will hold your people in my heart."* [1]

Suddenly, new light streamed through the stained glass window. The reds and blues were vibrant. His light, so bright and marvelous, covered me. And I knew again, faithfully-gratefully, I was not alone. I don't have to *feel* whether God is with me, I just know that He is.

> *"When Jesus spoke again to the people, he said,*
> *"I am the light of the world. Whoever follows me*
> *will never walk in darkness, but will have the light of life."*
> *- John 8:12 (NIV*)*

Since I was a little girl, I have known God has wanted to use me as His voice for peace, a channel of love. I'm not sure if I have lived up to it, but I have heard Him calling. I lift up my prayers for others and now for me, up to the heavens. That is what I have been called to do. Sifting through all the worries of life, it has taken years to fully respond to the call. But here I am. And I know what love is, and I know that I know. He is Love.

> *"Then I heard the voice of the Lord saying,*
> *"Whom shall I send, and who will go for us?*
> *And I said, "Here I am; send me!"*
> *- Isaiah 6:8 (NIV*)*

---

[1] *"Here I Am"* Dan L. Schutte
© 1981, OCP Publications, Oregon Catholic Press
www.ocp.org
Publisher Acknowledgement of Fair Use

Amen, Amen

Our prayer life continued and increased that first summer. Danny began ending prayers saying "Amen, Amen," after Ian and I had said "Amen." We giggled and thought it was special the first time. Then, I realized that he was embracing it as his signature sign off. Danny always had *just one more question* before lights out. One evening before bedtime, he needed to know what *does* "amen" mean. I had been taught in parochial schools it meant, "I believe."

Merriam-Webster's Collegiate® Dictionary, Eleventh Edition defines *amen* as, "used to express solemn ratification (as of an expression of faith) or hearty approval (as of an assertion)."[1] It may be used at the end of a prayer, but I know for sure it is only a beginning.

Ian and I get such a kick out of Danny's genuine routine. Now that's an oxymoron! After each prayer throughout the day we squeeze each other's hand as we bow with sweet anticipation of his double amen. Hugs and laughter follow, always.

I wondered if I could find any double amen in the Bible. Instead of doing a word search I thought I'd wait for God to reveal them. And He did . . .

> *"Praise be to the LORD, the God of Israel,*
> *from everlasting to everlasting.*
> *Amen and Amen."*
> *- Psalm 41:13 (NIV°)*

And . . .

> *"Ezra opened the book. All the people could see him*
> *because he was standing above them; and as he opened it,*
> *the people all stood up. Ezra praised the LORD, the great God;*
> *and all the people lifted their hands and responded,*
> *"Amen! Amen!" Then they bowed down and worshiped*
> *the LORD with their faces to the ground."*
> *- Nehemiah 8:5-6 (NIV°)*

Ezra taught the Law of Moses.

---

[1] "By permission. From *Merriam-Webster's Collegiate ® Dictionary, Eleventh Edition* ©2014 by Merriam-Webster, Inc. (**www.Merriam-Webster.com**)."

A Little Less Than God

Danny's bedtime gives us a chance to snuggle and to discuss things he's wondered about.

Some nights I let him know that I love them deeper than the ocean and wider than the sky. And Daddy does too. "Jesus loves you even more," I share. Danny questions, "So then He loves us bigger than the galaxies and all the planets?" I nod yes.

> *". . . what is mankind that you are mindful of them,*
> *human beings that you care for them?*
> *You have made them a little lower than the angels*
> *and crowned them with glory and honor."*
> *- Psalm 8:4-5 (NIV)*

The night before the new school year began was filled with anticipation and hope. Squirming and giggling surrounded evening prayers. In my own bed, I prayed for this new school year ahead, as I had been doing for days. I felt His awesome love for my children, for me, for all of us. It was rich and powerful and comforting. It was so similar to how I feel about the kids. Yet, it was more.

When Danny asks about my love for him, he'll be the first to know I love him a little less than God loves him. Wonder what he'll ask tomorrow . . .

> *"See what great love the Father has lavished on us,*
> *that we should be called children of God! And that is what we are!*
> *The reason the world does not know us is that it did not know him."*
> *- 1 John 3:1 (NIV)*

Bigger

It was a picture perfect day; 80 degrees in September. It was awesome. Blue skies stretched across the ocean. The sand was warm, the breeze was delightful, and the waves were breaking. The summer crowds were gone.

I sat on the beach relieved the kids were back at school. Crying hours had commenced; I permitted my tears anytime between the hours of nine and two! Still reeling from the shock of losing my soul mate, I smoothed the sand beneath me as if shaping it would somehow help me straighten out my own life. I fell into September carrying this anguish and so much more.

I thought I walked with Jesus since I was a little girl, ever since I could remember. Now, I knew He was carrying me. There was no other way. A childhood friend spoke those very words to me soon after, a confirmation deeply needed. The ocean so blue lay silent before me. Talking to Jesus was easy, His Spirit always before me. On the beach, I whispered to Him, *the ocean looks so big*. The wind blew over the sand, and me.

Broken, I sat before this mighty God and His ocean. Quietly yet with familiarity, His voice responded, *"My Love for you is bigger."* *Thank you Lord*, I choked out. Finally, tears.

"Because of the Lord's great love
we are not consumed,
for his compassions never fail."
- Lamentations 3:22 (NIV)*

When September Ends

Ian was being tested for sleep apnea. Restful sleep hadn't come naturally to Ian - pretty much ever. The day was filled with gathering clothes, medicines, stuffed animals and toys plus my first meeting with Ian's teacher. *There I go again packing so much into one day.*

The meeting did not go well. The teacher was full of suggestions. I thought to myself, *been there, done that.* I tried to describe what Ian is all about. No teaching the teacher today. Her response, "I don't care what goes on after school, I just care that he is successful in the classroom." She went on to imply his behavior was attributed to the *changes* at home. It is great that at least our thoughts remain private. The brain is awesome. God is awesome.

I was thinking: Ian didn't sleep last night, I didn't sleep last night, and I had an unfamiliar destination ahead of me. She insinuated as she accused, "I know there's a lot going on at home." I was ticked but I needed to be balanced for both boys. So I let it go. *Was that me, letting go?* But oh yes, I made a laundry list in my head to respond, just not now. I knew God was holding my tongue because I was screaming on the inside.

No warm, fuzzy feeling here, just a realization of the kind of year that was stretched out for us. How sad that our educational system mainstreams special needs kids without necessary supports. But holds them to the same expectations of typical children. The tragedy is that some teachers want to blame not understand.

Leaving the meeting; I had to remind myself to breathe. *Save your energy girl for the night ahead, leave this battle to God.* Danny was having his first sleepover with his father and was unsure of the night ahead. So was I. *Sweet Jesus, keep him safe and sound.*

Bud and I left each other - again. We went our ways in separate cars, not yet routine for me in the four months that had passed. *Shake it out; this is the way it is.* This time, he took Danny. It was hard to watch him drive off with my baby; yes he was seven years old at the time, but still my baby. Ian was peeled to the window. The big orange sun set on another September day. I drove unsure of just about everything in my life. But for now, navigating Rt. 280 was priority.

Driving to new places always makes me nervous. The dark was not a welcome companion. Going further west, we passed the time by singing whatever song was playing on the radio.

The song *"Wake Me Up When September Ends"* by Green Day was getting lots of air play. We had driven for miles. Even our headlights played solo. Ian started humming at first. Soon he picked up the melody. We had a summer drought, but for me, it had been raining in my heart for months.

My sweet boy would be tucked in tonight with all sorts of machines and wires. Did he stop breathing in his sleep? Could this be another piece to the puzzle? Another day to be strong, to stay strong - *you have to keep going girl*, I reassured myself. *When will it stop hurting? When Lord?* My mind racing - *how am I gonna raise these sweet boys? Where? How? God, please stop these tears.*

Ian really got into the song. Head held high he stretched his voice. I was broken for him, for Danny and for me. Eyes back on the road again I wondered how long had I looked away. My prayer in that moment, *Be with me Lord, Be with me Lord, when I am in trouble and need.* Then calm surrounded me.

Ian leaned forward and said, "Mom, wake me when September ends okay?" I smiled ear to ear when I said, "Uh huh." Turning my hand back to him, palm up he put his hand in mine. That's my car signal for the kids: *I am here for you.* A sweet sigh came from the backseat.

The drive turned out to be pretty easy. Off the highway, hospital signs led the way. Sleep that would not happen lay ahead. A couple of times an hour, he stopped breathing, I could see him catching his breath. It stopped my heart. He settled down. Then his legs became restless. Somehow, we both slept a little that night. At 5:20 am the nurse began to unravel the electrodes and monitors. Since the boys were toddlers, we have greeted each other the morning of every new month in a special way. This day was no exception.

I kept my promise to Ian too. I woke him with, "Happy October." A new day of *becoming who we are*, who we are meant to be. A sleepy return followed, and then giggles. *Thank you Lord.*

> *"As the Father has loved me,*
> *so have I loved you.*
> *Now remain in my love."*
> *- John 15:9 (NIV)*

Dear Jesus

I feel so very strange today. I have been so humbled in these past few months. I feel weary Lord. My body is tired. And my head is full of to-dos. I know You have brought me through all of this, and so very gently. There are bad days I think I will never be able to wrap my arms around all that has happened. And then there are good days, when I just don't care to think. You have been my strength. You continue to bless me with family and friends who just are there when I need them. You sweet Jesus and Father God and Holy Spirit, Holy Comforter have always been there for me. And, I sing You praise, even when my heart is breaking. For every battle in my life, and there have been plenty, you have been the victor. You have pulled me through. I feel like I am going through my own birth again. Giving birth helped me to know the labor pains and the "get me outta of here" pleas. When Ian was stuck in my birth canal, and they had me propped up and twisted, I thought to myself, will they notice if I just get up and leave right now? That's how I feel now. But everyone will notice. And I can't give up. I just have to keep going, praying and praising You and raising my sweet angel boys. These children are the best, Lord. And You are the Best. Thank you.

I feel stripped like everyone knows all the ugly things of my life. I feel so helpless. And yet I know better. I know You go before me and around me always. You have carried me sweet Jesus. I give You thanks. I send roses to reach to the heavens to thank You. I know You know the beginning, the middle and the end of these sorrows. I praise You for all the blessings of these sorrows. They are many. I give my life to You. I put it into Your precious hands. I ask that You hold me, Danny and Ian this day and always. Help me to be the mother You want me to be. Help me to be the person in Christ You want me to be. I love You with all my strength, heart, soul, body and mind. With everything, I love You Lord; I feel Your presence. You are amazing. Thank You sweet and mighty Jesus, forever and ever, Amen.

> "This is to my Father's glory, that you bear much fruit,
> showing yourselves to be my disciples.
> "If you keep my commands,
> you will remain in my love,
> just as I have kept my Father's commands
> and remain in his love."
> – John 15:8,10 (NIV®)

Sweet Caroline

Danny's friend Jack has a sister. She is four years old. Her name is Caroline. She and her mom go for walks with Daniel, her baby brother. When it's time to gather Jack, she loves to visit for a minute or two.

Caroline goes to great lengths to find me dandelions, leaves from the fall foliage, or flowers she has found along the way. It cheers me so. It's as if her little spirit knows what a little of this or a little of that will do for Mrs. Baker. Caroline pronounced, "I *bought* these for you." Sometimes she timidly murmurs.

I share my joy of her thoughtfulness. Her eyes widen when I call her Sweet Caroline. Unfailingly, she hugs her mom ever so closely and twirls her strawberry-blonde hair. Her smile can brighten the dreariest day. And then off she goes, whispering to her baby brother or the wind.

The three of us close the door and I take in the wonderful gift she has brought that day. One season folds into another, and our Maker makes all things new. Again, Sweet Caroline playfully approaches with her entourage. Some days blessings come knocking, literally.

"But Jesus called the children to him and said,
"Let the little children come to me, and do not hinder them,
for the kingdom of God belongs to such as these.
Truly I tell you, anyone who will not receive the kingdom of God
like a little child will never enter it."
- Luke 18:16-17 (NIV")

Christ Before Me

Christ before me, beside me and always with me. I feel so happy lately, almost giddy. And it doesn't make sense. All the sorrows of these past months feel so far away. It is wonderful. God is Great! Christ in the box. The box that surrounds, guards my heart, my soul.

My life is Yours.

> *"Keep your lives free from the love of money*
> *and be content with what you have, because God has said,*
> *"Never will I leave you; never will I forsake you."*
> *- Hebrews 13:5 (NIV")*

Calling All Surrogates

I am going through another transition, another letting go. Beginning the divorce paperwork, glancing around at my possessions, I begin to divide my life away from my husband. And it hurts, again. It's a different kind of pain, deep and settled in my soul. This one I release to God. It is the only way.

"Come to me, all you who are weary and burdened,
and I will give you rest. Take my yoke upon you and learn from me,
for I am gentle and humble in heart, and you will find rest for your souls.
For my yoke is easy and my burden is light."
- Matthew 11: 28-30 (NIV")

I remember years ago, after thirteen hours of labor with Ian, his heart rate was dangerously low and my blood pressure was 80/58. Oh how Ian tried to arrive face up, but the doctors turned him around. Good Lord, the earth moved within me. Later, we would learn the umbilical cord choked his neck and shoulder. I felt like I was hanging off the birthing chair that effortlessly broke away from the maternity bed. My first thought was, *I gotta get out of here and fast.* Apparently, I was in transition when I plotted, *If I could just get off this chair, bet they wouldn't notice I am gone. Yep. That's what I'll do.* Yeah right!

Earlier, I reacted to the epidural. I burned on the inside. Listening to Enya had been such a comfort during induced labor. I made fast friends with the Irish anesthesiologist. He drew near often to check on the baby and me. For him, it was a bonus to hear lovely music from his homeland. For me, it was another sign of transition. What he must have thought when I grabbed him and said, "You'd better get the fire department here! I am burning up." I know crazy, right?

Ian was born at 9:39 pm, and was hurried down the hall onto oxygen. After what seemed a lifetime, they laid him on the table to check his vitals. The shouts of joy and applause were indescribable as we all witnessed his first cry back in the room with us. I don't know how popular it is today, but I remember a time when couples sought out surrogates to bring children into their world. As Ian was born after our 13th wedding anniversary, I understood that longing.

Transitions, you've got to love them, *not.* The sixth month of separation after 26 years was no better than the first few days. My childhood friend called and shared my tears. With firsthand knowledge, Kathy knew how tangible the pain could be. Her husband had left her with three young children. She had been ill. The abandonment was insurmountable. He was GONE. With Christ's love, she began again. I am amazed and encouraged at her strength. I pleaded with her, "You have to find me a surrogate." "A what???," she rang out. "I can't go through this pain. It hurts too much. I'll pay, I just don't want to go through all this. It is too much to bear," I cried.

Kathy may have been shaking her head on the other end of the phone, but her response was loving. "Don't you remember what you told me when Michael left?" she asked. "You have to go through the pain, to get past it," Kathy reminded. "Saying the words and living them are two different things," I thought to myself. Instead I insisted, "I want a surrogate!" I didn't want to feel anything anymore, much less face it all.

A year and a half has passed since that conversation. It brings a smile. How did I ever think I could not go through to go on? And wouldn't it be great if we could just pay someone to live our pain? How much does it cost? Here you go, take it all! Life doesn't work that way, or does it?

> *"Cast all your anxiety on him*
> *because he cares for you."*
> *- 1 Peter 5:7 (NIV")*

There is One who takes our pain and sorrow: Jesus. His Holy Spirit is the Great Comforter. Jesus paid the ultimate price on the cross to carry our sins from death into life.

> *"Humble yourselves, therefore,*
> *under God's mighty hand,*
> *that he may lift you up in due time."*
> *- 1 Peter 5:6 (NIV")*

No disrespect intended, I toss my cares to the heavens. *Okay Lord, here comes another one.* No longer do I cry out for a surrogate to take my place in life's troubles. This child of God has a Great Intercessor. That is the greatest news!!!

> *"And I will ask the Father, and he will give you*
> *another advocate to help you and be with*
> *you forever — the Spirit of truth.*
> *The world cannot accept him, because it neither*
> *sees him nor knows him. But you know him,*
> *for he lives with you and will be in you."*
> *- John 14:16-17 (NIV")*

Transitions can be good, they birth new things. I don't know what's next. Some days I feel adventurous about my new beginnings. Other moments, I am absolutely terrified. But I know the God of Love is here for me *now*. Our Heavenly Father already knows the cares I'm going to toss and the ones I hold onto for dear life, my unlovely tug of war with our Creator. Yet in this divine exchange, He releases new joys to me, beauty for my ashes.

Kneeling before my bed, I toss more than cares to Him who loves me the most, the Love that will not let me go. I close my eyes and imagine the world between us open. I send kisses and majestic flowers of gold to our Lord in His heaven above. I really do. In my mind and heart, I know He receives them. When I'm not too sleepy, I remember to send Him chocolates too! Sometimes, I feel God smiling and I fall into sleep.

> *"Cast your cares on the LORD*
> *and he will sustain you;*
> *he will never let the righteous be shaken."*
> *- Psalm 55:22 (NIV*)*

Go In Peace

We were driving to Ian's check-up after adenoid surgery. The rain was coming down in sheets. Ian loves music on the radio. He does not hold back. He always seems so free when he sings. We were nearing the bridge. The van shook in the wind.

One of the disc jockeys from a popular New York City radio station signed off early that afternoon with, "Go in Peace." Ian's emphatic response rang out, "to love and serve the Lord. Thanks be to God."

Thank you Jesus, I whispered. *Sunday children's sermons are sinking in, deep. Thank you Pastor Dean.* Ian and Danny beamed in the rain.

> *"Let my teaching fall like rain and my words*
> *descend like dew, like showers on new grass,*
> *like abundant rain on tender plants."*
> *– Deuteronomy 32:2 (NIV)*

Another Birthday

It wasn't my birthday but it was two days after what would have been our 23rd wedding anniversary. A bitter winter day reminded me whose I wasn't anymore. I was in the sunroom listening to worship music by Hillsong United. During that time, I couldn't always praise and thank Him. I chose to sit still in the quiet away from the boys. In my stillness, I prayed.

I was consumed with thoughts on the anniversary that had passed, upcoming birthdays for both Ian and me as well as Christmas. *How will we make it through the holidays, Ian's birthday, mine?* Then without warning but with mighty Love I heard deep in my spirit, *"Let him go, write the book I want you to write, and start a prayer ministry."* My initial response, again sassy, *is that all?* Then came silence. Oh boy, I did it again I thought. Receiving a directive from above, I knew what I had to do but it wouldn't be easy. *And why am I always sarcastic? Thank You that You love me for me.*

Silly as it sounds, in my spirit, not with words, I prayed, *I can't do any of this without You.* Then I thought, *the only way to do this is to give God my heart.* I can only speculate it was the Holy Spirit, the true Giver, that prompted me to do so and acknowledge that I had put Bud and the kids first, and not our Creator.

Times were a changing in our cozy room on that wintry night. In the quiet on my knees, I made a choice to give this beautiful Father, Savior, and Comforter, all of me. *This is my life, take it, go ahead, here is my heart. I am yours, Ian is yours, Danny is yours, yes, even Bud is yours. Whatever you say, every decision from here on is between us.* There was no fanfare; no window into the future appeared. I had known Jesus since childhood. But I never took the plunge into believing, without question, God's Love for me. I lived for my family, myself, then God. But oh I loved Him. In a twinkling of a moment, I knew that I could live for Him in this surrendering, and I did.

> *"And so we know and rely on the love God
> has for us. God is love. Whoever lives in love
> lives in God, and God in them."*
> *- 1 John 4:16 (NIV)*

It was still dark outside, the kids were being silly in the recreation room, but something inside of me had changed. Chaos and anxiety that pervaded my heart and very being were replaced with an indescribable peace. Strength and sureness overtook my regrets and fears. I felt different, new somehow.

I was reminded of images of both Ian's and Danny's births. Remembering the first time I held them, each of them two years apart, their tiny fingers, clinging, tugging, and holding on. I loved the sweet look in their eyes as I introduced myself to them. I remember telling them, "I am yours, and you are mine, I have loved you all along. I will love you forever." This all-consuming love made me weep when I first embraced my newborns. Was it now my time to be embraced in this natural, awestruck kind of love? *Does God really love me that much?*

> *"Jesus answered, "Very truly I tell you,*
> *no one can enter the kingdom of God*
> *unless they are born of water and the Spirit.*
> *Flesh gives birth to flesh, but the Spirit gives*
> *birth to spirit. You should not be surprised*
> *at my saying, 'You must be born again."*
> *- John 3:5-7 (NIV)*

This unshakeable, immovable, absolute, unconditional Love is how this mighty Creator loves those He created in His likeness.

These beautiful memories flooded over me as I faced our upcoming birthdays in this difficult year.

Maybe 30 minutes or so had passed, and it was time to gather the kids for our evening routine. As I rose from the floor, I knew I had many tasks that lay ahead. But I had one more thing to take with me. This newness, my starting over, had begun. It felt like a clean slate. Was this my true birthday, a time of restoration? It felt like 4th of July on that cold night. I felt free and it didn't enter my mind to question the feeling.

> *"Yet to all who did receive him, to those*
> *who believed in his name, he gave the right to*
> *become children of God —*
> *children born not of natural descent,*
> *nor of human decision or*
> *a husband's will, but born of God."*
> *- John 1:12-13 (NIV)*

I have heard people say or ask, are you born again? How did you know? When? Honestly I thought this was just gibberish, something made up. While my chronological birthday was a week away, I was letting go and beginning again with sureness of God's love for me. Could this be another birthday, or my true one? I wasn't naive; there would be more tears, angst, and uncertainty.

But I knew I would really, really never go it alone. On December 13th, I accepted this Trinity of Love's invitation to love me, walk with me, always be with me all the days of my life. It was sealed in a promise spoken to Joshua thousands of years ago.

I believe, I accept, I give my heart to you, I live for you, Jesus, Lover of my soul. Words of His Great Love were waiting to be written. The answer was yes! That night I knew whose I am, forever. I am His, and He is mine, embraced in His unrelenting Love, I was born again. Thank you Abba Father, thank you Spirit Divine, thank you Jesus, Love's Way.

> *"For to me, to live is Christ*
> *and to die is gain."*
> *- Philippians 1:21 (NIV*)*

Surrender

*Spirit of Life, Giver of Life, I must admit I don't always
understand you. But I have come to know your unconditional Love
for me, Ian and Danny. And, oh yes, I welcome your humor. This
unplanned role as a single parent raising a son with autism,
and another young man, no less extraordinary, took me
by surprise. Yet, nothing surprises you.*

*I am in awe of your timing and goodness, Holy Spirit. I pray my readers
will see Your Heart & Compassion. Somehow, miraculously,
you really do live and move and breathe in us. I am grateful.
In the depths of joy and yes, even uncertainty of life, remind me to surrender;
spirit to Spirit, deep to Deep;
my life reflecting yours alone.*

ON MY KNEES
2006

The Palms of His Hands

"Whoever dwells in the shelter of the Most High
will rest in the shadow of the Almighty.
I will say of the LORD, "He is my refuge and my fortress,
my God, in whom I trust."
- Psalm 91:1-2 (NIV")

Ian, Danny and I got through our first Christmas. We never had so much company. It was wonderful. The revolving door didn't just bring in the cold but lots of love, family and friends. We were blessed.

I was surprisingly giddy, especially when Tracey came for a visit. I had eaten gluten-free cookies Nancy purchased online. I started thinking what in the world is in them? I was not accustomed to eating so much sugar after being diagnosed with celiac the previous spring. New Year's Eve was quiet. The boys and I spent it with Gram and Grandpa.

Starting a brand new year in our new kind of normal did not bring joy. The kids were fidgety and making every excuse not to go to bed. I was short of patience. Getting to bed the night of January 4th seemed impossible. All they did was talk about Daddy. Daddy this and Daddy that.

My fuse blew and I blurted out, "Daddy has hurt me more than you'll ever know." It wasn't seconds before I wished I could grab back those awful words out of the atmosphere. But it was too late. Danny started sobbing and Ian wept quietly. I could have just torn my heart out right there, better yet, my tongue. What had I done? I screamed out my hurt and anger. *Not doing such a good job of surrendering to you Lord? How can I ever make it right with these sweet boys?* They are so young and don't deserve to be hurt like this, by me. How could I be so selfish? *Think girl!* I apologized but nothing felt right.

It was time for prayers, and Danny didn't want me near him. "Oh no," I pleaded, "I won't let you shut me out. I may have lost my temper but I love you so much. And, we're saying prayers even if we don't feel like it."

Before we prayed, in his sweet seven-year-old voice, Danny had questions. He asked if Daddy and I were divorcing. I said, "Eventually." He said 'brother' had told him after Christmas. Danny still calls Ian 'brother'.

They affectionately called each other that for years. Ian began calling Danny by name about the time of the move but Danny continues. He then wanted to know if we'll ever re-divorce.

I asked, "You mean re-marry?" He nodded beneath his dinosaur comforter with a shy nod. I told them it is normal to want that to happen, but no.

Danny asked if he was going to have a new Daddy. I reassured him that Daddy will always be his Daddy. I told them that we both love them each so very much, and that will never, ever change. How we all missed him. To myself I thought, *Not doing a good job holding it together am I? Oh my sweet guys, nope, not at all.* I reminded both of them it's okay to be sad and miss him, promising I want to know their feelings, and it was important to share their hurts.

Ian went on to share, "If Daddy remarries, I will be angry with her to the end of eternity." What did this little boy know of eternity? I told him, "If that were to happen, you couldn't stay angry that long." He remained defiant. I almost laughed. Grief and silliness mingled. *Father, You are here.*

Once again I spoke of my love for them and said, "Now it's time for prayers." Sleepy grins replaced the worry on their little faces. *Forgive me Father.* They settled under their covers.

I offered my plea out loud to God to keep my big mouth shut, take care of my kids first, and trust in Him and His ways. I apologized again before prayers. They forgave me; now I needed to forgive myself. Tucking them in with kisses, I held my tears in until I made it to the kitchen.

Before we had gone upstairs, I turned off most of the lights, except for the Christmas tree lights in the sunroom and candles in the kitchen window lit the dark. I made my way to the table. Sorrows and regrets seemed to mock me. I buried my head in my hands and cried. *It hurts so badly Lord. This is too much pain.* I needed to be held so desperately but instead stretched my arms across the table.

Head down, I was soaked in my own tears. I felt Him near when I heard in my spirit, *"I have you all in the Palms of My Hands."* He seemed to be reaching from the other end of the table. His Presence felt so real. If I lifted my eyes from the grain of the wooden table, our eyes would have surely met. Instead, I remained still and let Him hold me. *Father, I need to give myself to you, help me do that.* Feeling so wimpy, my pleading seemed endless.

"Because he loves me," says the LORD, "I will rescue him;
I will protect him, for he acknowledges my name.
He will call on me, and I will answer him;
I will be with him in trouble,
I will deliver him and honor him.

With long life I will satisfy him
and show him my salvation."
- Psalm 91:14-16 (NIV®)

In the quiet glow of Christmas, His Light and Peace prevailed. I wiped my tears and shook off the pain. It was time to press on. I readied the table for breakfast, made school lunches, and kissed the kids one more time.

I took in the stillness of my bedroom and wondered how many times must I surrender my hurt, anger, and fear to Him? I knew the answer, every day and then some. He gave me rest.

"For his anger lasts only a moment,
but his favor lasts a lifetime;
weeping may stay for the night,
but rejoicing comes in the morning."
- Psalm 30:5 (NIV®)

In the morning, my head was clear. I accepted His grace and was forgiven. I thanked our beautiful Creator, my refuge, my song. With a smile to greet the morning, I gave Him my joy and kisses before my feet hit the floor. Our journey began, again.

"See I have engraved you on the palms of my hands;
your walls are ever before me."
- Isaiah 49:16 (NIV®)

My Cup Overflows

The week that followed a Sunday blizzard was dark. Bud didn't come automatically to help shovel us out. By the time we spoke, much of the job was done - by me.

If there was ever closure, this was it. After all these years, even with the kids, he didn't show. I had been beating a dead horse. Believing in redemption, believing in hope this time, was foolish. I had no priority in his life.

It stung. Then it felt dead. I was empty. Tuesday, I drove to our local pharmacy to pick up prescriptions for the kids. I told the Lord how I felt. The man I loved all those years didn't exist anymore. It was ugly. I thought our love was beautiful, even sacred. Making phone calls to him about the kids was now a chore, a dread. I didn't even want to hear his voice. How far had I come? Only nothingness was between us. Nine months to birth distrust, a quick road to loss.

The emptiness is so deep. I desperately need you Jesus every day. You give me strength to carry on. You carry me. I know you do. But I feel completely empty.

My emptiness was vast. The light turned red on Route 35. And just like that, I heard, *"Now, I can fill you."* No, it's not like I no longer knew where I was. I was in a moment with God, but very much in this world. As I waited for the light to change, I sat in His grace.

When I hear His voice, His peace is so amazing. *He loves me.* He loves us all. He remembers me in this dying place. It is a love that holds no conditions, only joy. God is with me, and He is in me. There is no doubt we are children of God.

As the week pressed on, so did the hurt. Over the winter, Bishop T.D. Jakes preached a series about living in a dying place. I reached that desert destination. *I had arrived.*

I no longer believe in coincidences. God places people and things together at certain times in our lives. Whether we are ready to hear or learn from them, well that's another story.

It may sound strange to people who don't attend church, but I love going to church on Sunday. I love to thank God and seek what He has to say to me. I am on a mission to hear His voice.

The following Sunday, the first reading from Isaiah 43:18-19 began:

> *"Forget the former things; do not dwell on the past.*
> *See, I am doing a new thing!*
> *Now it springs up; do you not perceive it?*
> *I am making a way in the wilderness*
> *and streams in the wasteland."*
> *- Isaiah 43:18-19 (NIV*)*

Oh Lord, this wilderness is vast, I wept. So it seems everywhere I look. Yet, His love for me breaks through the pain.

Onto the gospel, we read about the great lengths a paralytic went to reach Jesus to be healed. He was carried by four men and lowered into an opening of a roof because the crowds pressed in on all sides. When Jesus saw his faith, He forgave his sins and commanded:

> *"I tell you, get up, take your mat*
> *and go home."*
> *- Mark 2:11 (NIV*)*

Pastor Dean unraveled the message of the gospel. In doing so, he boldly stated our choices - to live or to die, to choose joy or live in regret. *Did he know I was in a dying place?* He told us Jesus wants us to choose life! It *was* time to live again. And I knew it was Jesus' declaration to me when Pastor encouraged us all, "Go on, get busy living!"

Soon, we knelt before the altar for communion. Before receiving, I whispered to the One, *I am not worthy to receive you, but only say the word and my soul shall be healed.*

His presence covered me. I responded, *I am so grateful Lord that you love me in this moment.* As the kids received communion, God nudged, *"Don't you know? I love you in every moment."*

My turn, as pastor imparted, "The Body of Christ given for you." My cup, His Love overflows; my amen could not be contained.

> *"You prepare a table before me*
> *in the presence of my enemies.*
> *You anoint my head with oil;*
> *my cup overflows."*
> *- Psalm 23:5 (NIV*)*

No Turns

There were plenty of days when I just didn't know what to do first. I was afraid. So I put one foot in front of the other and began again. Coming to the certainty of the end of my marriage wasn't easy.

Many errands filled one particular day. As I drove, "No Turn" signs were everywhere. I had never noticed so many of them. I suppose you don't look for them unless you are contemplating turning. There they were on the highways, cross streets, you name it. There was no way to avoid them in my daily travels. Seven months after 26 years together, I was still trying to understand why, trying to ground myself.

So when my friend Sherry came for a visit in January, she noticed the signs too. "Sure are a lot of 'No Turns' signs around here," she said casually. "Yep," I replied, relieved it wasn't just me thinking the same. As we headed over the Cooper Bridge into Red Bank, she prodded, "No turning back baby!" We had a good laugh. But on the inside I was unsettled. The roadmap was anything but charted.

I need to hear God's word daily. Many times, I read from the Bible. Most times I listened to Trinity Broadcast Network, (TBN) while advocating for Ian. I remembered a portion of this scripture that Joyce Meyer had embraced for herself and continually shares, *"The joy of the Lord is my strength."* I whisper this prayer whenever I feel down or unsure.

> *"Nehemiah said, "Go and enjoy choice food and sweet drinks,*
> *and send some to those who have nothing prepared.*
> *This day is holy to our Lord.*
> *Do not grieve, for the joy of the LORD is your strength."*
> *- Nehemiah 8:10 (NIV")*

God strengthens me and gives me joy. Sometimes, my gift from Him is a really close parking space on a freezing, rainy day. Other times, it is not being annoyed by things that used to really irritate me. Most times, it is making it through the day in love, patience and laughter for my sons *and* me!

I have learned so much about the Father's Love from the book of Joshua. The seventh verse of the first chapter took me by surprise and makes me smile when I now see the signs that used to shout at me.

"Be strong and very courageous.
Be careful to obey all the law my servant Moses gave you;
do not turn from it to the right or to the left,
that you may be successful wherever you go."
- Joshua 1:7 (NIV)*

My initial response to the Lord's direction was: *alrighty then.*

Holding onto God and His ways for my life, I go forward. Actually, sometimes I try too hard to keep on the path. Yet, it is in the surrendering, giving Him my heart, that life becomes effortless.

"Have I not commanded you? Be strong and courageous.
Do not be afraid; do not be discouraged,
for the LORD your God will be with you wherever you go."
- Joshua 1:9 (NIV)*

I am seizing that promise to Joshua, for me, right now. The Lord is with me in this present moment and all of my tomorrows. *What Love!* Honestly, there are times when I am afraid, but it no longer paralyzes me from doing what needs to get done, because *He promised.* Our God, *with me wherever I go, amazing and true*!

Oh, and when it is time for the turns in my life, I know our beautiful Creator will already be there, in the before, in the turning, and when I have found my way, in Him.

"Whether you turn to the right or to the left,
your ears will hear a voice behind you, saying,
"This is the way; walk in it."
- Isaiah 30:21 (NIV)*

Though it doesn't seem nearly big or gracious enough, *thank you, thank you, thank you Lord . . . for everything. Amen. Amen.*

Bread of Life

I had learned that one of my brothers was diagnosed with osteoporosis, which I live with too. Tom had learned he had celiac disease, and thought I should get tested. My results were positive too. At last, I had an answer to why I hadn't felt well for years. Celiac usually causes painful stomach problems. In my case, the disease attacked my immune system.

Going wheat and gluten free was challenging, but after 12 years of doctors telling me "It's all in your head," I was relieved. I was always at the end of tired and was so hungry adjusting to this lifestyle change.

My body can recognize if I have mistakenly eaten a wheat/gluten or preservative I shouldn't have. Now, I get terrible nausea, similar to morning sickness. But it lasts only a few days.

Never giving it much thought, I continued receiving Holy Communion each Sunday. "The Body of Christ, given for *you*," Pastor Dean boldly announces to each member at the altar rail. Awesome, Jesus is for me and the bread does not make me ill, such divine protection.

There was a time when Ian would mostly growl at people as they greeted him in the snugness of the floor and kneeler. He would spend most services down there. I had faith that one day he would be upright. Today, he sits in the pew *and* receives Holy Communion. The peace growl is just a faint, somewhat "beloved" memory.

Although Lutheran now, my heart prayer remains: *I am not worthy to receive you, but only say the word and my soul shall be healed.*

I say amen for the three of us, one by one. This sacrament, so wonderful, this Savior, King of Endless Glory is mine. Jesus reminds us that we belong to Him. His life is in us. This hymn sings His treasure:

> *"By your hand you feed your people, food of angels, heaven's bread.*
> *For these gifts we did not labor, by your grace have we been fed.*
> *In this meal we taste your sweetness, bread for hunger, wine of peace.*
> *Holy word and holy wisdom satisfy our deepest needs."*
>
> *"Christ's own body, blessed and broken, cup o'er flowing,*
> *life outpoured, given as a living token of your world redeemed,*
> *restored."* [1]

I am privileged to be a communion assistant. It moves me to see such light and love for our Savior on the other side of the altar. Blessed and sometimes broken, we come as little children, waiting to receive what we can never earn. Some come rich, some poor, some prominent, some others barely noticed, all changed forever in this breaking of the bread.

Nourished, we return to our pews redeemed and restored, His Love covering, this song sending:

> *"Send us now with faith and courage to the hungry, lost and bereaved.*
> *In our living and our dying, we become what we receive."* [2]

Thank you Father.

> *"Then Jesus declared, "I am the bread of life.*
> *Whoever comes to me will never go hungry,*
> *and whoever believes in me will never be thirsty."*
> *- John 6:35 (NIV")*

[1 & 2] *"By Your Hand you Feed Your People"* text by Susan Briehl, music by Marty Haugen

Tissues

It was March, and it seemed like every Friday since his father left, Danny, then eight, curled up on the sunroom couch and began to sob for his father. Something about the end of the week and the sunroom prompted his tears. Nine months after his father left, this particular Friday was different. Danny wanted to attend his school's talent show.

We went to the show and arrived one-half hour before its start. The auditorium was already packed, so we sat in the second to the last row. Danny kept pointing out his friends, sitting front and center.

We had to leave at intermission, because the kids needed to be in bed by 10:00 pm. Bud held long-awaited tickets to *Lion King* on Broadway for the next day. Years ago, I had this wonderful "picture" of the four of us, my parents and my mother-in-law. We would take a limo and dine in Manhattan after seeing the show. *What was I thinking?*

Upon our arrival home, hats, scarves and sneakers were thrown in every direction. A quick bedtime snack preceded Danny's all too sad Friday ritual. He wept in the sunroom. He began to sob and with every tear: "I miss Daddy, I miss him. Don't you?" he begged.

I took a deep breath and prayed. I curled up next to him and breathed in as much air as my lungs could handle. I hugged him, kissed him and began my honest yet repetitive words about how much Daddy loves him. He got mad and took off for the living room.

Meeting Danny there, I held and rocked him. I prayed. I need to do that pretty much always. *How can I make this child stop crying over his father, Lord?* Something came over me. I asked, "Wasn't Daddy getting really cranky when he lived with us just before he moved out?" And then I ever so gently imitated Bud's grumpiness. Danny laughed out loud.

I went on, "Doesn't Daddy spend more time with you than ever before?" His little hands released his head just enough to give a nod. Ian kept shushing him, saying "Baby brother, it's alright. There, there." With every brush of his shoulder came another wail. And I mean, wail. This is going well, I thought, not. Ian had retrieved the tissue box five minutes before this latest outburst. Danny's heart was breaking, and I could not allow either one to know mine was too, for them and for me.

What am I going to do? I looked at my watch. Then, I tapped it. Then out of my mouth came something so shocking even for me, "Danny Baker, you have two minutes. You have a father who loves you with all his heart; you see him all the time and he provides for you. It's not the best situation, but we're going to make the best of it." *That felt good, I said to myself.*

For a moment, I forgot Ian takes everything literally. No sooner were the words out of my mouth than Ian's feet hit the floor. He scooped up the box of tissues. This was no ordinary mission. I said no more tears and, he assumed the command would do.

With lightening speed he returned them to kitchen counter top, tossed the messy ones, and rejoined Danny sitting there with mouth wide open. Ian stood and eyed me for what was next on my agenda.

"Wait a minute. You are timing me?" Danny yipped. Ian hovered. In disbelief, he rang out, "You're timing how long I can cry?" "Yep," is all I could say. Never looking up, I brushed my jeans as if crumbs were scattered and said, "It's okay to cry once in a while, for a little while and get it out. Then, it's time to get moving and get on with life." *There, done, please God!*

> *"He will swallow up death forever.*
> *The Sovereign LORD will wipe away the tears*
> *from all faces; he will remove his people's disgrace*
> *from all the earth. The LORD has spoken."*
> *- Isaiah 25:8 (NIV®)*

Ian paced. He sought Danny's next move. Danny began to lift himself. A smile emerged on his round face. The trail of tears was no more. Tissues were indeed put away. Dreamland beckoned. The three of us sweetly yielded. *Father, thank you, again and again.*

> *"Do not be stiff-necked, as your ancestors were;*
> *submit to the LORD. Come to his sanctuary, which he has*
> *consecrated forever. Serve the LORD your God,*
> *so that his fierce anger will turn away from you."*
> *- 2 Chronicles 30:8 (NIV®)*

God's Face

My youngest seeker is none other than Danny. One question rolled into another as Danny asked, really inquired, "Have you seen God's face Mommy? Do you know what He looks like? You must know!"

Danny thinks I am his theological go-to person. Not! Little do they know how much I learn *from them* each and every day.

He was so close to *my* face that day with his inquisitive eyes. Danny played with my hair as his questions swirled around me. I smiled and thought, I've been wondering the same questions all my life. I have been seeking His face, always imagining, never sure.

> *"Seek the face of the Lord and long for Him:*
> *He will bring you His light and His peace."* [1]

I answered, "I don't know what God looks like. But once I saw Jesus healing Grandpa. It was many years ago. I only saw His back. But I knew it was Jesus."

He wondered, "I'll bet Jesus looks a lot like God. God's His Father right?" "Right Danny," is all I could say. This lovely mind is always at work. I sighed on the inside.

I shared my recent dream of God's face. He was Love, just Love and Joy and Peace. Danny just stared. I told him that no one has ever seen God's face and lived. He fumbled, "Whaddya mean?" I said, "It's important to seek God's face and His will for our lives but that we won't see God until we go to heaven." This was followed by a huge pause. "Wait a minute; I have to die to see God's face?" He begged, "That doesn't make any sense. That can't be." Deep theology with an eight-year-old at 9 o'clock in the morning wasn't on my agenda.

I did what any other mother would do in that moment. I sent Danny off in search of his brother. He sighed, "Okay." Before he took to the stairs of the attic bedroom, he peered over his shoulder. He was still seeking the questions unanswered.

I promised I would search what the Bible says about God's face. He had my word, then off he scooted! My Bible search of 'God's Face' turned up over 50 scriptures. I have yearned to see the face of our awesome God. To see Him would be brilliant.

51

Taking a break in my writing to tend to Ian's occupational therapy exercises, I wondered about all these passages. Before returning to the computer, I turned on the television and caught the end of The Reverend Billy Graham's Classics.

It was a crusade in Nova Scotia some thirty years ago. The Rev. Graham spoke about how Jesus seeks us. He calls us to be His own.

How incredible that God does the seeking. Jesus is not the past tense but ever present, Omni-present. He IS the Alpha and Omega. The All-Powerful, King of Kings and Lord of Lords calls us to be His.

> *"You did not choose me, but I chose you and appointed you*
> *so that you might go and bear fruit*
> *—fruit that will last—*
> *and so that whatever you ask in my name*
> *the Father will give you."*
> *- John 15:16 (NIV")*

We are blessed to be His. We long to see His face because HE loves us. *Thank you Father God, Sweet Jesus, Holy Spirit, Holy Comforter. Thank you!*

> *"The LORD appeared to us in the past, saying:*
> *"I have loved you with an everlasting love;*
> *I have drawn you with unfailing kindness."*
> *- Jeremiah 31:3 (NIV")*

Searching **www.BibleGateway.com**, I found these Scriptures about God's Face in the Old & New Testaments in the New American Standard Bible, (NASB): [2]

Genesis 32:30
Genesis 33:10

Exodus 33:20-23

Leviticus 17:10
Leviticus 20:3
Leviticus 26:17

Numbers 6:25-26

Deuteronomy
31:17-18
Deuteronomy
32:20

1 Chronicles 16:11
2 Chronicles 7:14
2 Chronicles 30:9

Job 33:26
Job 34:29

Psalms:

4:6
13:1
22:24
27:9
31:16
34:16
44:24
67:1
69:17
80:19
88:14
102:2
105:4
119:135
143:7

Isaiah 8:17
Isaiah 54:8
Isaiah 59:2-3
Isaiah 64:7

Jeremiah 18:17
Jeremiah 21:10
Jeremiah 32:31

Jeremiah 33:5
Jeremiah 44:11

Ezekiel 7:22
Ezekiel 14:8
Ezekiel 15:7
Ezekiel 39:23-24, 29

Hosea 5:15
Hosea 7:2

Micah 3:4

Matthew 26:39

Acts 6:15
Acts 20:25

2 Corinthians 4:6

1 Peter 3:12

Revelation 6:16
Revelation 22:4

---

[1] *"I Have Loved You,"* Michael Joncas
© 1979, OCP Publications, Oregon Catholic Press
www.ocp.org
Publisher's Acknowledgement of Fair Use

[2] "Scripture researched from the NEW AMERICAN STANDARD BIBLE ®, Copyright © 1960, 1962, 1963, 1968, 1971, 1972, 1973, 1977, 1995 by The Lockman Foundation."

Doors

Another beautiful blue sky July day. It was Monday.

The doctor called and said a new surgery was needed: last time, hernia, this time, ovarian cysts. Monday afternoon I met with my lawyer. She said that after the divorce I would lose the house. Last week, the school district wouldn't place important facts into an evaluation plan needed to get Ian help at school. The evaluation was in jeopardy. Now the district was calling. The fight for Ian's peace and my sanity was in full gear.

Getting out of the shower on Tuesday, I felt the words my dear Uncle Tommy had written soon after Bud left. They were words his mother, my grandmother, spoke in times of crisis. "It is always darkest before the dawn," he shared. The words spilled onto me as I toweled myself dry.

It was simple and clichéd, but could my dawn be coming? It had been so very dark. His light shines through the darkness. That darn to-do list kept growing: occupational therapy for Ian, lots of cub scouts activities for Danny, guidance from our family therapist, the divorce mediation proposal for Bud, and more medical tests were added.

When I prayed His spirit whispered, *"I can't open a new door unless you close this one."*

The boys were out for their Wednesday dinner with their father. The week was enough. No surprise I broke down and wept when my childhood friend called. Nancy, who has known me inside and out since the age of five, let me cry, but not for too long.

"You know Vic, God will open a new door when you close this one." She went on: "God closes one door and opens another. He always does." Keeping me grounded she asked, "When will he be bringing the kids home?" Gathering myself I told her, "Really soon." A face full of tears would set off more emotions in the boys.

Nancy, the strong one, a survivor in her own right, urged me to wash my face, get my smiles and hugs ready for kids. We ended the conversation. I splashed water on my face and was gently reminded me of His mercy. My friend spoke to my heart, my Savior spoke to my spirit. I felt doubly blessed. The kids always return home expectantly. They race to the door, singing, ringing the bell, knocking. They wait for me to open the door and they beg to be swooped into my arms. Absolute silliness erupts as they arrive home. Beautiful. Tonight would be no different.

> *"Here I am! I stand at the door and knock.*
> *If anyone hears my voice and opens the door,*
> *I will come in and eat with that person, and they with me."*
> *Revelation 3:20 (NIV)*

Dawns, doors and mercies, new each day for us, and it's all for the asking. God is Awesome.

> *"Lift up your heads, you gates; be lifted up,*
> *you ancient doors,*
> *that the King of glory may come in."*
> *Psalm 24:7 (NIV)*

After writing this passage I got ready for bed. A little past midnight, I peeked into my "Grace for the Moment" by Max Lucado. There, my new day's entry lay for August 26th. He quoted:

> *"You have begun to live the new life,*
> *in which you are being made new*
> *and are becoming like the One who made you."*
> *Colossians 3:10 (NCV)* [1]

And it gets better. Lucado spoke of Jesus the Shepherd who looks down at the sheep standing at the door, "Can I come in? . . ." The Shepherd beckons, "Come in, this is your home."[2]

I am home wherever I go. Thank you Lord.

---

[1] "Scripture taken from the New Century Version®. Copyright © 2005 by Thomas Nelson, Inc. Used by permission. All rights reserved."

[2] Used by permission. *"Grace for the Moment,"* Max Lucado, Copyright © 2000 by Max Lucado, Thomas Nelson, Inc. Nashville, Tennessee. All rights reserved.

Comings & Goings

Every morning one of us is running late, tripping on sneakers, backpacks or whatever is in the way. Weighed down by their coats and backpacks, the kids wait for me. I see them bumping each other, flying this way and that. They're laughing loudly as I run from brushing teeth to squeezing into my shoes.

Motion ceases at 8:40 am. We huddle at the front door for our morning hug to go. I grab my guys and wish them a great day. Then we hold onto each other. I pray over them, "Sweet Jesus, please bless my boys' comings and goings all the daylong with fun, safety, learning, knowledge, adventure and protection, in Jesus' name." We kiss. Then they screech, "Amen, Amen!" When the door flies open, the race to the bus stop begins.

"The LORD will keep you from all harm—
he will watch over your life;"
- Psalm 121: 7 (NIV")

It touches me to see another mom at the bus stop bless her children with a sign of the cross on their heads, lips and hearts. As with my guys, off they run onto their waiting bus.

How I know my Redeemer Lives!

"The LORD will watch over your coming and going
both now and forevermore."
- Psalm 121:8 (NIV")

The Dream

It was the second week of school. Monday morning Ian bounced down the stairs instead of his typical stomp through the kitchen. "Mom, I dreamed I was riding my bike. It was so much fun," he shared, rummaging through cereal boxes. "It must mean you're ready, honey," I offered. Almost eleven, he shrugged his shoulders, but his eyes told a different story. The day moved along and I wondered if the dream remained in Ian's thoughts.

September afternoons seem to fade into night so quickly as fall approaches. At least three times a week we try to walk the neighborhood together. Walking moves into talking.

That evening, the night was beautiful. Ian shared again about his bike dream. This time, he was excited. "Mom, I was so happy!" My soul smiled. The chill in the air persuaded him to bury his hands deep in his pockets. He looked up and said knowingly, "I'm gonna make it a goal." "Good for you, pal, it won't be long now," I urged. We headed home.

From then on, we didn't speak of the dream. Sunday, his father visited. The summer-like day lent itself to outdoor play. Ian and Danny took turns shakily balancing on their bikes. Danny would not ride because his brother couldn't. As he waited his turn, Ian spun around in the driveway. One foot on a pedal, his other foot scraped the pavement.

On the way out to run errands, I found Ian with his Dad practicing in the street. "I just can't balance," he said with incredible frustration. He stopped a hundred feet from me looking so defeated. "Close your eyes Ian. Remember how great it felt to ride, remember you could do it in your dream," I encouraged. Then, I prayed, *Father, be with him.*

He squeezed his eyes shut and then opened them with determination. Placing both feet on the pedals he biked to me, never stopping. It was awesome. Ian was riding his bike. The smile on his face was as wide as the sky above. I whooped, hollered and clapped. He leaned over the bike and hugged me, but not for too long. I raised my hands to the heavens and whispered, *thank you.*

The family across the way came out of their house, cheering him on. Another friend ran to congratulate him. Ian stopped only for a quick celebration of pink lemonade and Oreos. This childhood milestone had been realized.

The afternoon was hot but the smell of crisp leaves was in the air. Autumn would have to wait one more day. I thought how life is such a balancing act of knowing when to hold on and when to let go. Ian had to do a little of both that day.

I wondered how long our heavenly Father watches and waits. Jesus' nail-pierced, precious hands are outstretched, an open invitation of His love. I know He waits for me, but I have trouble letting go; I resist. Almost daily, I have to surrender to the Lord, to His plan and purpose for my life. I stumble, fall, wanting to do life my way. Yet, through it all, I know He is with me.

Something amazing happens when I give my day to Jesus. My cares turn into joy; my worry is replaced with peace. When I place all of me in His hands, let's just say mercy and love chase me down.

When I notice white knuckles on the handlebars of my life, I will remember Ian's victory. Even if I have to do it on purpose, I will let go and gain everything.

"Whoever finds their life will lose it,
and whoever loses their life for my sake will find it."
- Matthew 10:39 (NIV)*

Not Danny's Day

The beautiful autumn day was meant for hiking. Danny, along with his fellow cub scouts, were scheduled for a walk: Danny's official first hike. Ian and I planned on tagging along that warm Friday.

The knock on the door would change our plans. Dinner was cooking; Halloween decorations covered the living room. My agenda included packing for the kids' first-ever road trip to Disney the next day.

"Mrs. Baker?" one of two women asked. "That's me," I replied. After saying they needed to speak with me, I was informed they were from DYFS, the Division of Youth & Family Services. *Did I hear right?* Stunned, I opened the door, transforming into 'fight or flight' mode. After I asked them for identification, they dug in their cases. They took so long, I suddenly thought, "Am I being robbed?" So I locked the screen door. They shouted, "You have to let us in." Still stunned, now shaky, I opened the door. I have since learned my Fourth Amendment rights, but then I was very naive. This is special education in America!

I just about fell over when they announced they had received a child welfare complaint against me. *Me? The Division of Youth & Family Services?* They began spilling out the allegations. Realizing the school district was the source, I told them I would show them all my reports. Going up five steps to the office, they did not trust in my return. Suddenly they were behind me, peering in and out of the rooms.

Panic set in when I turned, and they were in my face. Bud had told me where he was working that day. There was no way he could get here quickly. Pulling the curtains to see if her van was in the drive, I saw Lisa, my neighbor, was home. I called; she came running. Thank God!

The very day before I heard in prayer, "*I will always be with you.*" Another warning given to me, yet another time for me to be clueless. My actions and decisions as a parent were now under investigation.

> "*What, then, shall we say in response to these things?*
> *If God is for us, who can be against us?*"
> *- Romans 8:31 (NIV")*

Listening to the preachers of TBN, I heard this and other scriptures about fear and evil during that week.

One daunting charge stood out among the several school-related allegations. "Ian has too many doctors, receives too much therapy and takes too much medication. There is nothing wrong with him." The school district left out that Ian has several medical conditions stemming from developmental delays. They never told the investigators Ian was diagnosed with PDD-Autism.

"No weapon forged against you will prevail,
and you will refute every tongue that accuses you.
This is the heritage of the servants of the LORD,
and this is their vindication from me,"
declares the LORD."
- Isaiah 54:17 (NIV)*

As they ruffled through medical reports and school evaluations, one of the investigators questioned, "Why are they doing this to you?" After months of purposeful delays, withholding student records, violations aplenty of Ian's rights and our parental rights, I had had enough. Two weeks prior, I had written the Child Study Team, stating I would contact the State Department of Education and file complaints if this continued. Another blow in my life I never saw coming. Geesh, another time I did not listen to God's nudging.

Lisa retrieved the kids from school. They returned home to their tear-streaked, visibly shaken mother. Bridget, another neighbor, took Ian for quite a while, as Lisa gathered Danny with other scouts for their hike. Seeing the same women from school, the kids were quiet, not knowing what was happening. Neither did I. There was only painful silence between us that afternoon. For me, words would not come.

Gratefully, Danny attended a monthly support group for siblings of Down syndrome and autistic children at Family Resource Associates (FRA). One summer, he had the chance to share *his* story and perspective on life with Ian in a newsletter. Here are some of Danny's thoughts . . .

"Even though I am the little brother, I act a bit like the older brother because I try to take care of him and his moods . . . I still worry about him and want to keep checking on him."

This was to be Danny's day. No matter how much I tried to carve out special time for Danny, autism took center stage, again. I phoned Bud when DYFS left. He arrived as soon as he could. The dinner I was cooking before their arrival, was burned, as was the corning ware. We sat in disbelief. How could I be accused of being a terrible mother to Ian? After our marriage ended, I knew to praise God and thank Him in advance, for protecting us through this uncertainty and providing strength for what lay before us.

Bud played with the kids, and I found readings from that Sunday prior. I felt imprisoned in yet another circumstance I did not plan in our lives.

"To the Jews who had believed him, Jesus said,
"If you hold to my teaching, you are really my disciples.
Then you will know the truth,
and the truth will set you free."
- John 8:31-32 (NIV®)

I knew the truths of my life. And, I knew the truth of Ian's needs must be told.

"But when he, the Spirit of truth, comes,
he will guide you into all the truth.
He will not speak on his own;
he will speak only what he hears,
and he will tell you what is yet to come."
- John 16:13 (NIV®)

In this world, truth is precious and rare. Jesus and His love for me was the only truth I could embrace that night.

By now, washing my face and replacing tears with make-up was second nature. Serving dinner and readying for the trip to Florida were priorities. The next morning the boys and Bud began their adventure. I started calls to Ian's doctors and therapists. Choking out the events of the previous day, I remembered Dr. Creflo Dollar's words that week on TBN, "Remember whose you are when you are in the time of crisis. You are a child of the Most High God." *Yes Lord, I am hurting, but I am yours.*

The November chill returned Sunday morning. Making my way to the altar to assist in communion, I trembled inside pleading to Him, *Lord be with me, please.* I began offering the cup, "This is the blood of Christ, shed for you." Time moved quickly and warmth returned. Concentrating to *not* spill the wine, the communion song played, the beautiful notes of the piano, the lyrics:

"Blest are you who suffer hate all because of me.
Rejoice, be glad, yours is the kingdom, shine for all to see."[1]

I fought back the tears, I felt so violated, for love's sake.

"Blessed are those who are persecuted
because of righteousness, for theirs is the kingdom
of heaven. Blessed are you when people insult you,
persecute you and falsely say all kinds of evil against

you because of me. Rejoice and be glad, because great
is your reward in heaven, for in the same way they persecuted
the prophets who were before you."
- Matthew 5:10-12 (NIV)*

Fighting the hurt and the anger, I gave in, believing all would be well.

The investigator called on Danny's birthday nearly four months later. The boys were off from school because of an ice storm. She apologized for putting me through the ordeal when our family had gone through so much to support Ian. "The last person you needed at your doorstep was me," she quietly admitted. I told her she was just doing her job. Her last name happens to be Lamb. Two weeks after the DYFS incident, Ian became eligible for special education. With the help of an awesome Advocate from the ARC (a nationwide support organization helping people with intellectual and developmental disabilities), we reached a six-year goal. (Little did we know it was only a little step closer to the true help Ian needed. We continued to provide private therapies and supports for years.) The ARC Advocate's last name, Logan, means to go through the valleys. Lamb came together with Logan in this small yet true victory for Ian.

"Even though I walk through the darkest valley,
I fear no evil, for you are with me;
your rod and your staff, they comfort me."
- Psalm 23:4 (NIV)*

The All-Knowing, ever present Lamb of God has led us out of lonely and frightening valleys of our lives. Into His immeasurable truth and safety, He beckons.

Broken, I arrive, changed forever rejoicing, actually celebrating time *and* again.

---

[1] "Blest Are They" by David Haas

Advocate

Ian was hurting himself by pulling out his hair, eyebrows and lashes when overwhelmed. He was pulling his cuticles down his fingers, until raw.

Although documented by the school nurse, his teachers *didn't see it*. They insisted these behaviors were just happening at home. Without a behavior plan or classroom strategies in place, his self-injury behavior escalated. Anyone with challenging disabilities needs a plan. Ian's challenges were scoffed at as non-existent.

While I suspected what educational advocates are, I had never understood their power. I reached out to a school mom, Margie, who had used the support of an educational advocate for her son. It was very successful and he got the classroom help he needed.

Margie then referred me to Stephanie, her son's advocate, who I called immediately. Stephanie returned my call, but informed me her job had changed. She referred me to an advocate from our local ARC, Sarah. We hit it off immediately. She listened as I poured out my failed approaches, understanding my son's needs.

We had spoken once before the DYFS incident. Although she had previously given me her home phone number, I left my tearful message at work about the allegations. Sarah happened to retrieve messages that weekend and called me from home.

Her steady, knowing voice was the assurance I needed that I was going to get through this ordeal. Our Advocate was armed with the knowledge of the law and experience in motivating and collaborating with school districts. I knew through Sarah, Ian's life would change for the better.

> *"And everyone who calls on the*
> *name of the Lord will be saved."*
> *- Acts 2:21 (NIV")*

Sarah knew the way through, around and out of our challenges. Our helper had arrived. Sarah was not just a guide but an intercessor. God works in pretty awesome ways. I cry out to God, and He hears my call. It's not magic; it's Love.

> *"All this I have spoken while still with you.*
> *But the Advocate, the Holy Spirit,*
> *whom the Father will send in my name,*

will teach you all things and will remind you of everything
I have said to you. Peace I leave with you;
my peace I give you.
I do not give to you
as the world gives. Do not let your hearts be
troubled and do not be afraid."
- John 14:25-28 (NIV")

I have advocated for Ian since he was identified as a child with special needs at the age of five. Conscientious about learning the special education process, I opened myself up to listening and absorbing as much as I could. Veteran moms were the most generous with their sharing. Every day I found out how much I didn't know.

What I acquired from Sarah was far different. She taught me to look at every milestone Ian had accomplished and our work leading to that goal. In order to move forward, we needed to let go of the insults and intimidating experiences. Sarah emphasized profiling Ian and his immediate needs. It helped us see what Ian accomplished.

With home exercises, private therapy and maturity, Ian began meeting milestones. It didn't matter the months or years it took to catch up. Because of God's amazing grace, Ian is bright, talented and a joy.   With each developmental delay, God moved us this way and that, finding new solutions, new reasons to hope. For each new puzzle piece, like strengthening muscle tone or building physical endurance, God aligned us with the next *helper* in our lives.

God didn't forget Danny in the process either. Encouraging Danny as often as I could, the siblings group at FRA was a godsend. There, Danny shared his hurt and frustration. In a loving space, other kids with brothers and sisters with intellectual disabilities knew exactly what Danny was feeling. He received loving support and had fun too! FRA helps our community with early childhood programs, family support, creative recreation experiences and adult programs. Their mission: PossAbilities for people with disAbilities.

If we turn to God, not shutting Him out of the secret hopes of our hearts, the doors of life swing wide open. We no longer stand in isolation, or get in the way of His love.

"Today, if you hear his voice,
do not harden your hearts as you did in the rebellion,
during the time of testing in the wilderness,"
- Hebrews 3:7-8 (NIV")

Thinking back on Ian's eligibility and Individual Education Plan (IEP) meetings, Sarah acted more like a barrister. In England, that is a lawyer who can practice as an advocate, particularly in the higher courts. Higher, hmmm? For Ian, Sarah questioned, negotiated, even reprimanded!

As we continue advocating on Ian's behalf, we kick our failures and pride behind us. Meeting Ian's evolving needs, we adapt our goals for him and press on.

> *"My dear children, I write this to you so that you will not sin. But if anybody does sin, we have an advocate with the Father— Jesus Christ, the Righteous One. He is the atoning sacrifice for our sins, and not only for ours but also for the sins of the whole world."*
> *- 1 John 2:1-2 (NIV)*

The Father sent the most humble, loving, nevertheless powerful intercessor, the Holy Spirit of Jesus Christ. When I truly surrender these cares, my worries no longer loom like black clouds. Instead, blessings become bigger than the obstacles. I begin once again to thank Him for Ian, Danny, health, home, even for those who have hurt us . . . I *get* to say *thank you* over and over again.

We believe our lives are in God's hands. The Lord orchestrates the entrance of many *helpers* in our lives with His perfect timing. I find myself again, a beggar in waiting, worshipping, and definitely pressing on.

> *"For I know the plans I have for you," declares the LORD, "plans to prosper you and not to harm you, plans to give you hope and a future."*
> *- Jeremiah 29:11 (NIV)*

Note: See "This is Special Education?" p. 74 and "Burden of Proof" p. 80.

Daughter of Zion

I have never heard Father God call me by Vic, Vicky or Victoria. Not even a
Hey You echoed. But I have read and watched many preachers share their
intimacy with God. For years, in prayer, I have heard *O, Daughter of Zion.*
I never quite understood, but I really remembered the "O!" As I have come
to truly understand God's love for me and for us all - I realize how wonderful
it is that He calls <u>me</u> "daughter."

Through my years, I have read portions of the Bible in addition to
participating in Sunday services. To say I was ever Bible literate was a stretch.
This year much has changed. I cling to the Word of God as I cling to Him.
For they are one in the same. And so I searched and found my answer about
Zion. I sort of figured Zion had to do with Jerusalem. And then I found
this . . .

> *"Awake, awake, Zion, clothe yourself with strength!*
> *Put on your garments of splendor,*
> *Jerusalem, the holy city.*
> *The uncircumcised and defiled will not enter you again.*
> *Shake off your dust; rise up, sit enthroned, Jerusalem.*
> *Free yourself from the chains on your neck,*
> *Daughter Zion, now a captive."*
> *- Isaiah 52:1-2 (NIV*)*

And . . .

> *"Rejoice greatly, O daughter of Zion;*
> *shout, O daughter of Jerusalem:*
> *behold, thy King cometh unto thee:*
> *he is just, and having salvation;*
> *lowly, and riding upon an ass,*
> *and upon a colt the foal of an ass."*
> *- Zechariah 9:9 (KJV)*

Oh!

*I am a daughter of the Holy One. How humble this makes me feel - how Magnificent and
Awesome is HE! Thank you, thank you Father.*

> *"Therefore my people will know my name;*
> *therefore in that day they will know*
> *that it is I who foretold it. Yes, it is I."*
> *- Isaiah 52:6 (NIV*)*

Joy Unspeakable

I never needed my legal marriage certificate during my life with Bud. It was summer and I found myself calling the county courthouse to retrieve it for my first-ever digital photo driving license. I saw the irony but not the humor. This token need of the 21st century was just one more reminder of failure and loss.

Timing is everything. At prayer time, I stumbled onto St. James' urging, "Count it all joy." *Joy, joy? I wanted to scream. How is that possible Lord?* I read on . . .

"Consider it pure joy, my brothers and sisters,
whenever you face trials of many kinds,
because you know that the testing of your faith produces perseverance.
Let perseverance finish its work so that you
may be mature and complete, not lacking anything."
– James 1:2-4 (NIV")

A few months prior, I was speaking with my friend Leigh Ann about what I had heard in prayer. Her husband was hospitalized; the family was coping with their own turmoil. We shared our faith. It was a deep cold, clear day. Looking at the crystal blue sky and wondering if spring would ever arrive, I spoke of God's comforting words to me, "*I will give you joy unspeakable, daughter of Zion.*"

Leigh Ann encouraged me to take God at His word. I believed when I felt anything but joy. Daily whispers to the Father, *the joy of the Lord is my strength*, brought peace from time to time.

"Be joyful in hope, patient in affliction, faithful in prayer."
– Romans 12:12 (NIV")

Every day I gave more of myself to Him, the anger, the hurt, the worry, eventually everything. Slowly, purposely, He changed me. God loved me, revealing: "*You belong to me.*" How blessed I was to hear His assurance. The Father, precious Son and Spirit became my life. When the pain was so raw and aching, I heard, "*Let him go.*" When I cried out, *Lord, I need you desperately*, His comforting whisper, "*I am with you always,*" kept me sane. In my stillness, the Lord brought peace to me.

What were once tears of sorrow turned into tears of thanksgiving and yes, even joy. I saw His presence in each season and the changes in my own. His light shone in Danny and Ian and all the loving people in our lives. Everywhere I looked I found God! *I chose joy.* Was I kidding myself? No. Each passing day, God's love for me became more evident and tangible.

I am not naive; devious, hurtful people are everywhere. For every one of them, God sends plenty of loving mentors, friends and healers of the body and heart.

In prayer on September 6th, hearing *"The fight will continue, I am with you - there will be endless joy"* was notice for the months to come.

I chose joy, I chose life when it hurt the deepest, when He promised, *"This hurting sacrifice is all I ask of you."*

How fitting it was when the reader spoke the next morning at Sunday service, *"I call heaven and earth to witness against you today that I have set before you life and death, blessings and curses. Choose life so that you and your descendants may live, loving the Lord your God, obeying him, and holding fast to him."*

> *"This day I call the heavens and the earth as witnesses against you*
> *that I have set before you life and death, blessings and curses.*
> *Now choose life, so that you and your children may live*
> *and that you may love the LORD your God,*
> *listen to his voice, and hold fast to him.*
> *For the LORD is your life,*
> *and he will give you many years in the land*
> *he swore to give to your fathers, Abraham, Isaac and Jacob."*
> *- Deuteronomy 30:19-20 (NIV)*

I am His child. He has loved and freed me. I live with Him, in joy. Joy, once off in a great distance, is now real.

I Come with Joy, a Child of God

> *"I come with joy, a child of God,*
> *forgiven, loved, and free,*
> *the life of Jesus to recall,*
> *in love laid down for me."* [1]

Trust

Abba, thank you for creating everything, including me. Thank you for this wonderful life. You are our protection, refuge, go-to Guy for everything. It wasn't always that way. But I am changed. Today, I begin the day with you, race through the hours you have graciously provided only to fall into bed once again knowing your sweetness. Abba, knowing that you are, and you are holding Danny, Ian and me ever so gently is enough. Thank you my song, my life, my everything.

GETTING UP
2007-2010

The Chalice

One cold January night in 2007, I woke from a dream. I suddenly found myself sitting up in bed. I had been watching a woman walk across my bedroom carrying a beautiful chalice. It was so difficult to shake off the dream because it was so real. Though very strange, I wasn't frightened.

I still had hurting days but not every day. The nights however, were different. Having been held during the night for nearly 23 years then suddenly not, took a lot of getting used to. I resorted to fluffing pillows to fill the emptiness of too much space.

Months had gone by, and complex ovarian cysts continued to grow. One doctor urged a hysterectomy. I found a new doctor. How odd that they were named complex. That was the definition of my life. The man who was once the love of my life was gone. Poof! Ian was still struggling in school. Danny missed his father terribly. Moving to a new town and home had come with its own adjustments.

The past September my gynecologist reported that one cyst, measuring three inches had simply disappeared. Other cysts seemed to hang on despite my insistence for them to vacate. Family and friends prayed. There were days I could actually feel their prayers. Love covered me. I can only describe it as grace. It wasn't anything I deserved, it was just an awesome blessing.

I continued to pray for healing for myself, and got on with the business of life. Palm oil, a heating pad and prayers were my response when I heard, *"Physician, heal thyself."* Hearing that did sound bizarre. Then I thought, if this is the Lord, the Great Physician, how can I not listen?

Back to the chalice. It was silver inlaid with the deepest blue. The cross stood out. The woman was none other than my gynecologist. Awake it was almost amusing, but in the dream it was very solemn.

Dr. Tsong is a petite, Asian-American. She is kind and strong. Imagine, this petite woman holding this chalice boldly before her. With dignity and joy she glided across my bedroom. She didn't seem to notice me. She walked with authority knowing what she held was sacred.

Two months later during an ultrasound, the technicians whispered: "That's where the complex cysts were," and they turned to each other in disbelief. I was in no position to see the screen, as if that were an option. I quietly prayed and waited. It took two weeks for Dr. Tsong to get the results of those quarterly ultrasounds. "Well, Victoria, I don't know how to tell you this but the complex cysts are gone. It is rare. It is strange," she went on to say. Three doctors had told me that they could only be removed by surgery. They could not be shrunk nor be dissolved.

She went on to tell me a small cyst that remained was about three centimeters but could be dissolved. I took a mental break from the conversation and prayed up, *Thank you Jesus, thank you!!!*

"I don't know what to say," Dr. Tsong concluded, and I offered, "our prayers were answered; it's God."

It wasn't time to share my dream, my cup of salvation. Weekly, we share in the communion feast with our congregation. The server bears the wine and speaks, "the Blood of Christ shed for you." The chalice, the cross, the healing love of Jesus . . . for me, you, for all of us.

Thank you Jesus . . .

> *"I love the LORD, for he heard my voice;*
> *he heard my cry for mercy.*
> *Because he turned his ear to me,*
> *I will call on him as long as I live.*
> *The cords of death entangled me,*
> *the anguish of the grave came over me;*
> *I was overcome by distress and sorrow.*
> *Then I called on the name of the LORD:*
> *"LORD, save me!"*
> *The LORD is gracious and righteous;*
> *our God is full of compassion.*
> *The LORD protects the unwary;*
> *when I was brought low, he saved me.*
>
> *What shall I return to the LORD*
> *for all his goodness to me?*
> *I will lift up the cup of salvation*
> *and call on the name of the LORD."*
> *- Psalm 116:1-6,12-13 (NIV®)*

I Praise You Lord.

This is Special Education?

The ARC was gathering family stories in their battle to reverse the "Burden of Proof" legislation. Parents bore the responsibility of proving that their child's education plan was insufficient, but that required expensive experts and attorneys in order to prove their case. Unfortunately, many parents were unable to obtain an appropriate program to meet their child's academic, social, and emotional needs. This was our family's story:

"He can do it." "The district is only obligated to provide an adequate education." "Take that thing out of your mouth; you can't bring toys to school." "Is he playing a game?" "I don't know if any kids in this school have autism." "Ask Ian to aim to throw up in the wastebasket." "Don't expect we are going to change anything because your son has food allergies." "There is nothing wrong with your son." "PDD is not autism." (PDD, Pervasive Developmental Delay.)

"Ian, almost twelve, has Asperger's Syndrome, a high-functioning form of autism. Over the years, these comments flowed effortlessly out of the mouths of administrators, principals and teachers. Identified in pre-kindergarten as a special needs child, services and the pursuit of Ian's challenges were dropped, even hidden, beginning in kindergarten. Determined to understand all of Ian's needs, notwithstanding academic, we embarked on an agonizing and often degrading journey. We became stuck in the perplexing world of special education.

Six years after he was identified by Elizabeth, New Jersey's "Early Childhood Initiative," Ian was made eligible for special education, but that didn't mean he received meaningful services. Four Child Study Team evaluations later, Elizabeth and his current school district refused to accept (much less document) Ian's neurological disorders. They do this because they can. The burden of proof is on parents.

In addition to his autism, Ian is challenged with several developmental disabilities, including ADHD, auditory and visual processing, sensory integration, impulsivity and anxiety.[1] Ian also lives with asthma, a severe allergy to peanuts/nuts and irritable bowel syndrome.

Years of writing letters, e-mails, meetings and phone calls have been combined with pouring over the PRISE (Parental Rights in Special Education), Wright's Law and the New Jersey Administrative Code until they have become a part of me.

I have watched Ian be misunderstood because of inappropriate behavior and his inconsistent ability to understand social cues and interact with children his age. His grades are consistently inconsistent, and he keeps getting pushed ahead. Fall entrance exams reflect his inability to retain information over the summer.

Overwhelmed when he cannot process new information or as changes occur in his routine, he resorts to pulling out his hair, eyelashes, brows and cuticles until they are raw. And the district and school just don't see it. The first day of standardized testing in 2006, Ian left school without much of his right eyebrow. Last year, vomiting episodes from an allergic esophagus caused dismissal over a dozen times.

My concern about all those missing lessons went where my previous pleas have gone - to his file.

With four state mediations, over 50 violations of Ian's educational and our parental rights, a handful of complaint investigations, nearly $100,000 in private therapies, we have not reached our goal. Where is Ian's free and *appropriate* education?

The obstacles, semantics, retaliation, and intimidation from school districts are relentless. Yet, I became relentless as well. Some of the obstacles: I have been threatened to retract a statement or else; I learned that Eden Autism Services was locked out of scheduled classroom observation at Ian's school; I was told I could not give Ian's brother medicine in the nurse's office; and I was unable to review a proposed evaluation plan unless I signed consent beforehand.

I have been chased down by Ian's Case Manager trying to retrieve Ian's file I was not supposed to read after finding a district e-mail that said: "These parents are HOT, get quick evaluations, must be anxiety." Never mind the nearly four-month child welfare investigation or the almost slam-dunk eligibility meeting when four evaluations had not yet taken place much less reports made available.

Trenton's words of wisdom were "Get into that meeting or they'll have it without you." Through the years we have been blessed to have the support of a SPAN (Statewide Parent Advocacy Network) mom, pro bono services of an attorney, and an advocate. But it's not enough. We do not have equal footing on the education playing field. Several policy loopholes in the evaluation, mediation and complaint processes give districts the home court advantage. Special education law does not address unethical behavior or misconduct. The government cannot legislate morality.

The petition to our May mediation request was responded to with statements that were misleading, taken out of context and some, just untrue. I have learned to let go of the insults, and focus on Ian's classroom needs rather than defend untruths. This is not about me, it's about Ian. In March, I had to choose my battles; one was to address a classroom incident that caused Ian great distress. That competed with scheduling an IEP meeting when the district sent a final plan before we had even met. And, at the same time I was pleading for help for more evaluations, so he wouldn't hurt himself again.

When the State Department of Education looks away, school districts thumb their nose because they know most families cannot afford a $10,000 legal retainer. Filing complaints result in losing precious time with special children and their siblings who need their parents. The added bonus for contacting the Office of Special Education Programs is retaliation. It's a lose-lose situation.

I am not naive to think many students like Ian have gone before him. And too many children with all kinds of disabilities are left behind right now with parents fighting similar battles. The day before his fifth grade classes ended, Ian cried out, "I would rather die than go back to school."

That remark pierces me; I can't let this one go. School districts must be held accountable to all students. Parents must be released from the ridiculous burden of proof. *My* tears have never been enough. The future of the bravest and most awesome children I know depend on *yours*."

My little boy suffered so much, and no matter how I fought, I could not protect him. I recounted his pain as I condensed his school experiences into this neat, three-page package for legislators. This testimony was originally sent to ARC for review. What was their response? Bud and I were invited to testify before the N.J. Senate Education Committee in November, 2007. Wow! *Thank you Jesus!* After writing this testimony, I searched the Word . . .

> *"Place the cover on top of the ark and put in the ark*
> *the tablets of the covenant law that I will give you.*
> *There, above the cover between the two cherubim*
> *that are over the ark of the covenant law,*
> *I will meet with you and give you all my*
> *commands for the Israelites."*
> *- Exodus 25:21-22 (NIV")*

---

[1]ADHD stands for attention deficit hyperactivity disorder, a condition with symptoms such as inattentiveness, impulsivity, and hyperactivity. The symptoms differ from person to person. Source: **www.webmd.com**.

Dance with Me

We were married thirteen years before having children. When the boys were toddlers, we danced to music, silly songs from Sesame Street to Sinatra swing. We so enjoyed being parents, we would swarm together and dance in the middle of the living room, with or without music. We had our own family rhythm.

Bud would gather one of the boys, and I the other. Then we would embrace and dance. It was just joyful cuddling together. The boys looked forward to Daddy joining in the fun, mostly after a long work day or before heading out in the morning. Sometimes, Bud scooped both boys in his arms, and I joined the three. Other times when Bud and I danced, the kids would push and yank until four became one.

These days, the boys and I are in growing disagreement of songs on the radio. One the guys love is "Dance with my Father," by Luther Vandross. Just writing the title brings a lump in my throat. If I hear the first notes of this song and am driving solo, I quickly change the station. That is called self-preservation. When together, Danny sits quietly dreaming. I am sure he remembers. Ian sings to the top of his lungs. Gripping the wheel, I pray for my sweet boys *and* for the song to be over.

The week of that first new year without my best friend, we saw the most surprising sight. Driving home from church, at least 50 birds appeared to be dancing. Flying above and in front of us, they seemed to lead the way home. Swooping and gliding, this was not the usual v-formation. There was a clear leader of this flight performance. We watched, oohed, and aahed. The birds turned and we laughed in amazement.

They led us to the bridge crossing the Navesink River. Soon they scattered and were gone. Those were the days I prayed, "Help me in my unbelief." So many times in prayer, I had heard, *"All things shall be well."* I felt like I was living someone else's life. I did not give God my confidence, much less my trust.

When I saw this leader of the dance, I thought of Him. God wants to bring us joy, laughter and peace. He leads us. I go my way, caught up in the steps of my life; I forget to dance.

A long time ago, I gave Psalm 23 to my memory. In between the happenings of my life, I needed His comfort. Reciting this prayer of David, a King, a sinner, a man after God's own heart, helps my busy mind to rest. Breathing and living it draws me ever closer to the Lord.

> *"The LORD is my shepherd, I lack nothing.*
> *He makes me lie down in green pastures,*
> *he leads me beside quiet waters, he refreshes my soul.*
> *He guides me along the right paths for his name's sake.*
> *Even though I walk through the darkest valley,*
> *I will fear no evil, for you are with me;*
> *your rod and your staff, they comfort me."*
> *- Psalm 23:1-4 (NIV")*

Last night, Danny worked on his autobiography for class. He considers me his very own "spell-checker." Together, we reviewed his writing. Returning the assignment to his folder, with wisdom beyond his years, he shared, "You probably know more about me than I know about myself."

Quietly, I agreed. He was off to play with Ian. That is how God must feel about all of us. He knew us before we were born, molding and shaping us. And if we allow Him, He continues creating masterpieces all over creation.

The Master of the universe also loves us more than the depths we could ever imagine. He knows when we lose sight of Him and when we beg to have Him at our side. No failure, no heartache, no sickness, no job loss, not even death, can separate us from His love. My favorite apostle, St. Paul, wrote:

> *"No, in all these things we are more than conquerors*
> *through him who loved us. For I am convinced that neither death nor life,*
> *neither angels nor demons, neither the present nor the future,*
> *nor any powers, neither height nor depth,*
> *nor anything else in all creation,*
> *will be able to separate us*
> *from the love of God that is in Christ Jesus our Lord."*
> *- Romans 8:37-39 (NIV")*

My parents celebrated 50 years of marriage in August, 2007. As I write, it is just a few weeks past that festive weekend. Ian was rock n' rolling on the dance floor. His free spirit bounced and moved to the beat of any fast music. My sweet Danny Boy tugged at me as I mingled with family and friends. The music slowed. Danny politely asked, "Would you like to dance with me, Mommy?" How could I resist? Taking my hand, he led me to the dance floor.

We didn't practice. Danny was a bit stiff, not sure where to place his hands and which way his feet should go. Trying to get him to relax and get in the groove, I noticed his glance at me. Danny held on tight, looking at me as if I was the only person in the room. He was so precious.

I was glowing in my nine-year-olds' love for me and mine for him. After their anniversary waltz, my parents were referred to as Fred and Ginger. My little guy and I were definitely not in that category. But his contagious smile lit up the room and my world.

Our family dance has changed, yet it's new and magical. The music is playing, our steps not quite sure. That's okay because we've got that rhythm. I haven't remembered smiling so much in years as I watch Danny's loving face.

Typically, the kids take my lead in life. That night was different. My sweet prince led the way. The Prince of Peace, the King of Kings calls me, leads me and I gladly follow. Joy has returned. King David danced before the Lord. Whichever way we sway, we have felt our beautiful Creator's deepest love in the lovely dances of our lives.

"There is a time for everything,
and a season for every activity under the heavens:
a time to be born and a time to die,
a time to plant and a time to uproot,
a time to kill and a time to heal,
a time to tear down and a time to build,
a time to weep and a time to laugh,
a time to mourn and a time to dance;"
- Ecclesiastes 3:1-4 (NIV)
A Time for Everything

Burden of Proof 2007

"Good Afternoon Chairwoman Turner and members of the NJ Senate Education Committee. My name is Victoria Baker. Thank you for this opportunity.

My son, Ian Baker, almost twelve, now in fifth grade, was diagnosed with autism at age seven. For two years prior to that diagnosis, Ian was identified as a child in need. However, despite our efforts, it took seven years from when he was first identified in 2000, to be made eligible for special education services, in March, 2007. And, if it were not for Governor Jon Corzine's intervention at the beginning of this school year, Ian would not have the education plan that was agreed to last March.

Ian's developmental diagnoses have never been accepted by his school districts. Respected medical experts have diagnosed his disabilities and allergies. However, these reports have been questioned and ignored. It would seem that Ian's Asperger's, life-threatening allergies and other disabilities take leave of him from the weekday hours of 9:00 am to 3:00 pm. What is essential is not visible.

I have watched Ian struggle, suffer, hurt himself, work harder than most kids ever have to, and be left behind time and again. I have sat with him and his tears under the kitchen table doing homework. I felt his anguish when he screamed out last June, "I would rather die than go back to school."

In these seven years, I have also watched our life savings depleted from all the financial burdens of private therapy. I have become a single parent. I have watched my youngest child become his brother's keeper, expressing his deepest worry that Ian's teachers won't know how to handle him. Will he hurt himself or another?

I have been disgraced and retaliated against by so-called professionals of this broken education system. We have endured ridicule by teachers, child study teams and administrators, and a nearly four-month children services' investigation. It hasn't simply been enough to prove, without success, my son's disabilities. I have had to disprove that I was a Munchhausen by proxy mother, as well as other educational allegations. Two other families in our small elementary school were also subjected to visits from DYFS. While this agency agonized over our case, a child was fatally stabbed at the hands of his mother in our county.

In pursuit of my son's rights, we have experienced these emotions while dealing with over 50 violations and four state mediations. We have been astonished, overwhelmed, appalled, stressed, devastated, frustrated, perplexed, disillusioned, and disappointed. Now, the only thing that overwhelms me is God's grace.

The Burden of Proof must be placed back on the shoulders of school districts across New Jersey. It must be made district-proof, in other words, air tight. No longer should administrators be allowed to deny services by denying diagnoses in the name of balancing budgets. Our district won't even accept its own findings and recommendations.

I have watched, powerlessly, as districts manipulate Chapter 14 of the NJ Code, and twist truths while I counter their semantics. All of which have left Ian struggling and hurting.

I implore you to release parents of the burden of proof. What more proof are we as parents expected to present, than the statements of accepted medical experts? How is it that a school district can accept a diagnosis from one of these experts for one child, but not accept it for another? My little prince needs you in this season of his life, as do all children with disabilities.

"I have not apprehended but one thing, forgetting those things that are behind me and pressing towards the goal, reaching to the things before me." These words from St. Paul are words I live by as well.

I have placed these incorrigible actions against Ian and our family behind me. Tomorrow, I press on to other educational battles. But today, Ian's future is before you. His disabilities are apprehended as invisible. I pray that you are able to see them.

Please take what is invisible, make it real, make it law until it becomes essential for all precious children. It is only with your heart that you can see what is very real. Thank you for this privilege."

The burden returned to schools when Governor Jon Corzine signed legislation in January, 2008! *Amen Lord, thank you!*

"Not that I have already obtained all this,
or have already arrived at my goal,
but I press on to take hold of that for which
Christ Jesus took hold of me."
- Philippians 3:12 (NIV)*

Lilies

I am in the trenches. Okay I'll admit it - I've been stuck in a pit of darkness and confusion. I know Jesus is the way, the only Way. The Way up and out has been pretty silent these days. Yet in all of my yesterdays, He had never forgotten me, no not once. So why is it so hard to hold on to Him? In these summer days of rain, I mutter, *I trust you God, I trust you God.* Walking through each room, doubt is the very air I breathe. Sometimes I whisper, and other times I speak out loud against visible odds: *God will supply all my needs.* And the kids give me the look, *there she goes again . . .*

> *"And my God will meet all your needs*
> *according to the riches*
> *of his glory in Christ Jesus."*
> *- Philippians 4:19 (NIV*)*

Thank you Lord, Ian is in the wonderful place of healing. Therapy in the form of Brain Gym exercises, Interactive Metronome, and natural supplements are soaking into his body and mind.[1] Peace has come with love and one-on-one instruction. Homeschooling was another unexpected yet sacred detour.

My divorce was delayed. New discussions have turned ugly. I just want it over, but there are so many decisions to be made and changes ahead. My prayers to God return as a knowing deep within, *"Take care of the children."* And, sassy as ever, I respond, *That's it? But what about the bills, Ian needs to be in a special school, but where are we going to live, how can I afford health care, how can I work and home school and care for Ian's needs? But, but, but . . .* I am exhausted during the day and wide awake at 2:00 am. There it is again, silence.

I search for St. Paul's boldness, *"I can do all things through Him who strengthens me."* In this ungodly hour, I just feel like a weakling. Every microscopic detail of the divorce agreement paralyzes me. How can I agree to all these changes for our lives? I hate that I am in this place in my life *and* that I am whining. Wrestling with God, I don't stand a chance. But *I want, I need,* keeps me awake until I give up: *it's Your way.*

> *"For no word from God will ever fail."*
> *- Luke 1:37 (NIV*)*

One morning I woke to the alarm clock set to music humming from Third Day, *"It's Alight,"* a beautiful song about trust, but I wasn't completely there yet.

Homeschooling, bills, activities for the kids, therapy exercises, financial and divorce planning fill my days. Father God, which should I do first? *"Finish the Book."*

No point in arguing, I grabbed pen with pad and headed outdoors. I began my draft of what I thought should be the final passage but nothing connected. I intended to write about my uncle, a vibrant and tender Franciscan monk who touched so many with the love of Jesus. Toward the end of Uncle Tommy's life, breathing while lying down was impossible. He would sit and watch movies to fall into sleep. Whisked off to Glory a year before, he never knew of my purchase of "Lilies of the Field" for him. Starring Sidney Poitier, a reluctant helper became a blessing to a small community while realizing his own blessings. Missing my uncle, I never opened the video intended to see him through his midnight hours, the video that arrived the 2008 spring day he died.

This summer, I received an open invitation to volunteer at a two-acre farm tract benefitting autistic children in our community. The founders, Barbara, Liz and Mai, of *OASIS tlc*, have helped me many times weaving through autism's unchartered journey. Weeding, watering and tilling the soil are all part of the chores. Ian weeded with peer buddies, while Danny and I worked together one evening. Most nights when Bud had the kids, I'd find peace there, in the quiet, good earth.

It was just a few of us on those hot, summer nights. One Monday, finishing a little after eight o'clock and trying with great effort to stand, I noticed Mai bustling. Loading her car, she excitedly pointed, "Look Vicky, in the fields, the lilies." My eyes locked into the blazing sky of pink that seemed to consume us; I muttered to myself, 'Of course, they are in the field.'

Already dancing past the gladiolas, Mai shouted, "You have to take some." Looking upward, I offered, *Guess you really want me to finish the book!* Not unlike an intimate secret between lovers, I was given this sunset gift. And yes, it also felt like a brick hitting my head. His voice so familiar, God is too much of a gentleman to say, *"Do you finally get it?"* This Love that will not let me go, assured me that evening of His mighty presence and sense of humor.

With gratitude, I gathered the handful of gaping flowers from the arms of this beautiful protector of autistic children. The scent of lilies, joy that could not be stifled, and His promise to be with me always, followed me home. Sleep was sweet that night.

"Therefore I say unto you, Take no thought for your life, what ye shall eat, or what ye shall drink; nor yet for your body,

what ye shall put on. Is not the life more than meat,
and the body than raiment?

Behold the fowls of the air: for they sow not,
neither do they reap, nor gather into barns;
yet your heavenly Father feedeth them.
Are ye not much better than they?

Which of you by taking thought can add one cubit unto his stature?
And why take ye thought for raiment?
Consider the lilies of the field, how they grow;
they toil not, neither do they spin:
And yet I say unto you, That even Solomon in all his glory
was not arrayed like one of these.
Wherefore, if God so clothe the grass of the field,
which to day is, and to morrow is cast into the oven,
shall he not much more clothe you, O ye of little faith?

Therefore take no thought, saying, What shall we eat?
or, What shall we drink? or, Wherewithal shall we be clothed?
(For after all these things do the Gentiles seek:)
for your heavenly Father knoweth that ye have need of all these things.
But seek ye first the kingdom of God, and his righteousness;
and all these things shall be added unto you.
Take therefore no thought for the morrow:
for the morrow shall take thought for the things of itself.
Sufficient unto the day is the evil thereof."
- Matthew 6:25-34 King James Version (KJV)

Three weeks later . . . pressing forward with the bickering and lack of negotiating . . . selling the house is on Bud's agenda. Ian is so isolated now, but at least he can ride his bike in the neighborhood. Staying home with Ian and Danny for ten years hasn't placed me in a position to purchase a home. Letting go of this home, a safe haven through many storms of our lives, will be devastating for my children. Bud wants to move on. I fear Ian will regress, and Danny, who has made many friends, will be crushed.

A few years ago in prayer I heard, *"Give me the house and I'll give it back to you."* Every night, we give thanks for the roof over our heads covering it with, *This is your house God, Your home.*

I am not sure if it's the divorce, turning fifty, menopause, or all three, but even church makes me want to scream. There, we don't find acceptance for Ian's challenges. To some, he looks disinterested, not trying, or even a bit lazy. People don't say it, but try to get him to straighten up, look alive, and participate for Pete's sake. Do I have to put a sign on his back, the big A? I am so tired of defending, explaining. Isn't church supposed to be a place of acceptance, of love? Increasingly, the glares from church kids are getting to me too. Ian, becoming more aware, senses the stares which make him more anxious.

Sharing my concerns with Lisa, she lets me know of a church that seems to really embrace families. After checking out the website, I visited without the kids. Lincroft Presbyterian (LPC), was just that, a loving, spirit-filled experience.

Summer sermons revealed the names of God throughout the Old Testament scriptures, one of the many, Jehovah-Jirah, God my Provider. Pastor Brian was teaching the children a song that ended, "He is sufficient for me, me, me." Even the prayer, Assurance of Pardon echoed, 'My Shepherd will supply my need, Jehovah is His Name.' More than ever, I needed to hear those words.

Three days remained until another divorce mediation meeting; my head was spinning. Pastor Brian asked the congregation, "What are you holding onto with clenched fists that God wants you to hold on loosely? God is asking us to treasure Him more than the things we have in our hands. Give God what you are holding onto, and He will return it to you." *I can run but can't hide, can I Lord?*

> *"Rejoice in the Lord always. I will say it again: Rejoice!*
> *Let your gentleness be evident to all. The Lord is near.*
> *Do not be anxious about anything, but in every situation,*
> *by prayer and petition, with thanksgiving, present your requests to God.*
> *And the peace of God, which transcends all understanding,*
> *will guard your hearts and your minds in Christ Jesus.*
>
> *I rejoiced greatly in the Lord that at last you renewed your concern for me.*
> *Indeed, you were concerned, but you had no opportunity to show it.*
> *I am not saying this because I am in need, for I have learned to be content whatever the circumstances."*
>
> *"I know what it is to be in need, and I know what it is to have plenty.*
> *I have learned the secret of being content in any and every situation,*
> *whether well fed or hungry, whether living in plenty or in want.*
> *I can do all this through him who gives me strength."*
> *- Philippians 4:4-7,10-13 (NIV)*

Christ's peace and love grounded me once more. Driving home, the Christian radio station, Star 99.1 FM, played a song that wasn't familiar, so I switched it off but quickly changed it back when I heard, "There's no God like Jehovah-Jirah." What a God!

I stretched my eyes toward Him with thanks and said, *I got it.* No sooner did I finish, the knowing spirit of the Comforter presented, *"I've got you."* I rejoice *that it is so. Thank you, thank you, thank you Lord.*

Mediation went wonderfully well with both of us letting go of things we had bickered about for a very long time. Trusting God, I am moving forward. We are coming to an emotional settling of the terms without more traumas. God is so good.

A new adventure is about to unfold for the three Bakers. I live my life thanking, praising and trying, not always succeeding, to be His light in this very wonderful and chaotic world. For me, putting God first has resulted in the most extraordinary relationship with our magnificent Creator.

Through the fragileness of our lives, in my becoming, God *is* the love of my life. Just when I thought it was me building my faith, this Author of Life showed me He has been the Maker all along.

Note: Years later, as I edit this passage for publication, we have far too many blessings to count. Bud has been a wonderful, loving, supportive father, and generous as well. Oh, and we have remained in our sweet house, God's home, of course.

[1] Brain Gym is an exercise movement program committed to the belief that "moving with intention leads to optimal learning." Interactive Metronome is a form of occupational therapy that supports brain and coordination through exercise. More on Brain Gym can be found in Recommended Resources on p. 134.

He Loves Us So

Ian was getting sick again. Tremors and belly pains returned. Was it fall allergies, anxiety, what could it be? Maybe just another transition. Autism has not been a welcome friend. *Please Father, not again.* Public school had started, and for the first time in nine years, he didn't attend. School had been such a disaster, we decided to home school him.

Many times I took it all upon myself. This time I trusted Him, completely.

> *"I lift up my eyes to the mountains-*
> *where does my help come from?*
> *My help comes from the Lord,*
> *the Maker of heaven and earth."*
> *- Psalm 121:1-2 (NIV®)*

Homeschooling Ian, now 14, I could see his needs more clearly. I knew he was safe and the incidents were weekly, not daily or as often as they had been. He was sniffling at the start of a fall season that persisted in its warmth through October. His allergist recommended new medicine.

Off to my annual mammogram in the fall of 2009, I planned to stop by the allergist's office to pick up a sample. I got my own surprise that day. Breezing through the mammogram and feeling really good six months after my lumpectomy, I got ready for an ultrasound.

As the radiologist began checking, she noticed the scar and said, "What nodule was removed?" My reply, "Whaddya mean, the one you found last fall, that one." The radiologist explained *that one* was still there and bigger than last year. I'll admit I didn't hear all that she was saying after that.

> *"You will not fear the terror of the night,*
> *nor the arrow that flies by day."*
> *- Psalm 91:5 (NIV®)*

Climbing into the van, I remembered the dream I had just a few weeks prior. I was flying. I know, flying solo, just me and the sky sounds really strange. But there I was soaring over a swimming pool. My scream as I flew was a bit primal. Do you ever wonder if you scream in real life as you dream?

If I did, this had to have the neighbors talking. In the dream, I noticed a huge, beautiful butterfly painted on the bottom of the pool. As I touched down onto the patio, a voice boomed from the heavens, "cancer free."

Waking from this dream, I wondered what that was about. Somehow, I knew to thank the Lord. Driving closer to the allergist's, the dream was a comfort. As I waited for the nurse to explain the dosage for Ian, a woman was leaving, sobbing.

Gerry, I would learn her name, made it to the parking lot a few seconds before me. I found a lipstick near where she had stopped and scooped it up thinking it might be hers. I approached her van. Rolling down her window, tears still flowing, she told me the lipstick wasn't hers. I yielded to our Maker's sweet nudge.

Asking if she was okay, duh, I thought to myself. "Can I help you?," spilled out of my mouth?" She smiled. Gerry told me she had just lost her Father and couldn't stop crying. She told me she was sorry. Waving it off, I told her I would pray for her. Then God urged me, "God wants you to know He loves you so. There'll be a time when the tears will stop. Cry when you need to, but not for too long. He really loves you so." She nodded then smiled, and I headed home.

I remember those kind of uncontrollable tears. I didn't believe it was going to be alright. "I can't bear it Lord," I pleaded. I asked Him to take the hurt from me. And, He did!

The Lord is close to the broken-hearted. That day was no exception. Turning on the radio to Star 99.1 FM, I began the short drive home. The sounds of the piano were clear, purposeful. Tuning in midway to a new song, *"How He Loves"* by the David Crowder Band, I was touched by God's timing.

How incredible! *Thank you Lord, You love Gerry and Ian . . . How I need you so desperately. But You know that - already. Please cover Gerry in her sorrow, Precious Jesus.* My heart praised Him.

Eleven days later, the nodule collapsed as the needle biopsy began. Cells captured were cancer free. Ian felt better; homeschooling, raking leaves, loving his younger brother went on, uninterrupted.

> *"But I trust in your unfailing love;*
> *my heart rejoices in your salvation."*
> *- Psalm 13:5 (NIV®)*

If God can bring peace to our chaos, He can do it for anybody. Yes, He does love; marvelously, wonderfully, all of His creation.

Bowing Daffodils

The spring of 2010 had such meaning. It is always a gift, sometimes a reward after a cruel winter. The second week of January had brought turmoil to our family. During open-heart surgery and the morning that quickly followed, we almost lost Mom, twice.

She was unrecognizable the evening of surgery with tubes covering her body, the respirator pumping and hissing. Three nurses huddled with stats at her bedside. We were told, "Go home and get some rest." We took turns entering the room filled with hanging meds, protruding tubes and my Mom.

My younger brother and I stood. I felt pulled in by the breaths of the respirator. Could this be her? Nearer to the bed I inched, *this wasn't Mommy, this is not my Mother.* This is another patient, we have the wrong room.

Certain I couldn't leave for the night until I knew it was her, I kept seeking. My brother brushed my sleeve and pulled me away at the moment I found her eyes. It was her. I remember gulping tears with one last look at the nurses.

That afternoon at 2:00 pm, we were taken to a room used for families of heart transplants *and* the bereaved. My sister, her youngest, grabbed me as I felt my knees give way. This couldn't be happening. "You're the strong one, you can't lose it on me now," she begged.

To myself, *girl, take a breath, so many close calls for Ian, breathe.*

> *"Turn to me and be saved, all you ends of the earth;*
> *for I am God, and there is no other.*
> *By myself I have sworn, my mouth has uttered in*
> *all integrity a word that will not be revoked:*
> *Before me every knee will bow;*
> *by me every tongue will swear."*
> *— Isaiah 45:22-23 (NIV)*

We navigated the hall and took up our residence in what felt like a life-proof room. Seeing my father staring into space, God brought me back to myself. Snacks and plenty of water were ushered in with quiet reverence. The aid shut the door and left. The silence was tangible. Deep into winter, spring felt a lifetime away.

Her youngest son first broke.   Between the tears, *we never should have let her go through with this surgery.* Her oldest, followed with his regrets. As my sister comforted them both, I choked out, *this is what she wanted, she decided.*

Three weeks passed; first an induced coma, then intensive and cardiac care brought emotional upheaval as she needed a pacemaker, transfusions, more tests, lungs drained. It seemed each day was greeted with new complications. I had my tears in the car, on the way to her and back home. Blessed with many caring friends and Bud, the kids were shuttled as I headed for the hospital.

All of us were hastily e-mailing and texting in the halls outside of intensive care. Trying to keep up with our lives, our mom's was delicately apprehended by aids, nurses, doctors but most of all, by God. The blizzard of 2010 would hold off until her very bumpy transport to a rehabilitation center.

Mom strained to speak, all but a whisper; her breath labored for weeks.

> *"Let everything that has breath,*
> *praise the Lord. Praise the Lord."*
> *- Psalm 150:6 (NIV")*

Praise Him even now? It was the only way.

She was overwhelmed. Her physical setbacks crushed her spirit. As I ached inside, for her, for Dad, for me, I searched His Word.

> *"As it is written: "I have made you a father*
> *of many nations." He is our father*
> *in the sight of God, in whom*
> *he believed—the God who gives life to the dead*
> *and calls into being things that were not."*
> *- Romans 4:17 (NIV")*

Every evening, after prayers with the boys, I called out to Him. *Mommy belongs to you! She is your child. You give life, strength, healing, peace and courage. I claim them for her because she can't. In the powerful name of Jesus Christ, Your Son, I praise you, I love you. Thank you Jesus, thank you Jesus.* I didn't remember falling off to sleep.

The driving didn't matter every day, then every other day, an hour to the hospital then onto rehab for two weeks. Even with record snowfalls, we managed to get out of the driveway. Ian sometimes shoveled snow onto Danny. It's funny now.

Thankfully, neighbors regularly helped dig us out. Miles and prayers meshed. The sounds of loving, uplifting worship music traveled with us on each highway. Weekdays during rehabilitation, we visited, homeschooled in the lobby, ate lunch as we moved.

"For in Him, we live and move and have our being.
As some of your own poets have said,
'We are his offspring.' "
- Acts 17:28 (NIV®)

It was cold and Ian didn't want to be there, but he never said so. I didn't know how else I could be doing this without Jesus. The staggering hurdles - eating, getting out of bed, standing up, walking were overcome. Returning home with support from a visiting nurse, therapist and aid, she flourished. Each day, more. Less naps, her laughter returned as she phoned others in need. Her voice and body grew stronger. Daily exercises, friends visiting, a spirit of gratitude hovers - *over all of us.*

Getting the van ready to take cooked meals and goodies on Easter Sunday, I decided to clean it. A mild Maundy Thursday prompted me to haul out the vacuum. As I reached across the middle seats, MercyMe's song, *"All Of Creation,"* settled inside of me.[1]

The words, "And every knee will bow . . ." wrapped around me. The music was just between me and God. I checked out my daffodils, so beautiful and enormous after the snows and heavy rains. They seemed to be bowing too, radiantly. Could it be?

With my work on the van waiting, I grabbed my boom box. Amazing I thought, as I walked past the daffodils. And what was playing? *"All Of Creation,"* was, of course. I seek you Lord, and you are here with me and for everyone else. *Thank you!*

Even the daffodils bow to you Lord. Maybe it was the harshness of winter? *Nah.* Creation just knows that it knows. You reign.

"Shout for joy to God, all the earth!
Sing the glory of his name; make his praise glorious.
Say to God, "How awesome are your deeds!
So great is your power that your enemies cringe before you.
All the earth bows down to you; they sing praise to you,
they sing the praises of your name.
Come and see what God has done,
his awesome deeds for mankind!"
- Psalm 66:1-5 (NIV®)

Easter Sunday, she greeted us at the door, without the walker. It was a very long Good Friday, nearly three months, followed by a spectacular Resurrection Sunday. We celebrated, cried, and laughed. Mom saw Easter!

We witnessed His promise, the miracle of Easter in her, and now, in His creation.

> *"And we all, who with unveiled faces contemplate*
> *the Lord's glory, are being transformed into his image*
> *with ever-increasing glory, which comes from*
> *the Lord, who is the Spirit."*
> *- 2 Corinthians 3:18 (NIV")*

Spring had shown up and shown off, in all of His glory.

> *"Splendor and majesty are before him;*
> *strength and joy are in his dwelling place."*
> *- 1 Chronicles 16:27 (NIV")*

---

[1] *"All of Creation,"* The Generous Mr. Lovewell, MercyMe © 2010 Produced by Brown Bannister & Dan Muckala, INO Records/Fair Trade Services.

Written by: Writers Brown Bannister, James Bryson, Nathan Cochran, Barry Graul, Bart Millard, Michael Scheuchzer, Robin Troy Shaffer, Daniel Muckala
Publishers: BANISTUCI MUSIC/SIMPLEVILLE MUSIC/WET AS A FISH MUSIC (CO-PUB)/WINTERGONE MUSIC.

Permission Granted by: Music Services Inc.

The Table Was Set

Susan called about the kids' sizes for the upcoming passion play. We laughed about how quickly kids grow. During family dinner that evening, the Lenten prayer was about the practice of "Making Promises a Holy Habit." As we discussed the disciples, Danny blurted out, "Promises, promises, like Peter right?" "And yes, how they needed to be forgiven," I added. Danny shot back, "again and again and again!" Sharing this tale, Susan and I were amazed at Danny's aged insight. Susan assured me that what he is hearing at church is sticking. I thought to myself, *It isn't disappearing into the atmosphere, thank you Lord.*

> *"Train a child in the way he should go,*
> *and when he is old he will not turn from it."*
> *– Proverbs 22:6 (NIV")*

Susan and I spoke further; both our families would be attending Maundy Thursday service. Before hanging up, she let me know the service was just beautiful. *Beautiful, a service of darkness,* how could it be?

Always listening to His Spirit, LPC had become our church home. New to the denomination, each church celebration is somewhat of a mystery, an anticipated adventure. This Maundy Thursday in 2010, we would learn, would be no different.

God's whisper, *"Amazing love"* quickly followed the next morning's scriptures and prayers for the day. *Beautiful, amazing, really Lord?* I questioned Him and settled for belief.

The car clock was nine minutes fast to cover my always needing just five more minutes. I know, playing with time never works. One of my new year's resolutions was to show up on time. Yeah, that wasn't working either. Every time we climbed into the van, the kids would complain, "Mom, we never know what time it is. Please change the clock!" "Oh sure you do," I responded pointing to the clock, "that minus nine minutes!" Promises, promises . . .

Spring ahead was a deal breaker. Do I push the old clock just an hour ahead or make the necessary adjustments? Moving the clock forward, I saved just one extra minute for me. *Didn't think I could invite Jesus into the plan.* I know, wimpy on all counts.

It was 7:29 pm when we skidded yet again, into church. Racing past the tender wood of the newly built narthex; I whisked the boys around me and into the sanctuary. There, everyone was seated. Time stood still. We had entered into a sacred place. Trying to quiet my mind and heels, I searched to find three seats together. I could always count on open space in the front when we were late. Ignoring the groans of the kids, we shimmied into chairs careful not to disturb other members sitting very, very close by.

Sunday prior, the sanctuary was lined with chairs on either side of the center aisle. That night, the beautiful transformation of a sanctuary into a banquet was breathtaking. Tables covered in white, one lined right after another with three set across in T-formation. Candles and bread, light and wine, newly familiar faces were before us. Pain and suffering were there too - held in Love.

> *"Therefore, I urge you, brothers, in view of God's mercy,*
> *to offer your bodies as living sacrifices, holy and pleasing*
> *to God—this is your spiritual act of worship. Do not*
> *conform any longer to the pattern of this world,*
> *but be transformed by the renewing of your mind.*
> *Then you will be able to test and approve what*
> *God's will is—his good, pleasing and perfect will."*
> *- Romans 12:1-2 (NIV')*

Where do I put my eyes? I don't think I've sat this close to anyone in years. The prelude was purposeful and somber; I looked at the program. Ready to close my eyes I heard, "Hey, Vic, hi!" Pastor Brian reached a wave to the boys and me. Waving and smiling back I thought, *What is he doing? Doesn't he know this is solemn, I mean solemn, Lord?* And just as I finished my pompous dialogue, God put on my heart. He's just being like Jesus. *Will I ever get it Father, the first time? Will ya help me, please?* Okay, I can close my eyes now. *Did I put Easter dinner in the frig?* If Ian could read my mind, he'd scream, "Focus woman!"

The service began with a call to remember Jesus' loneliest day. Jesus, our Savior, lonely? *I am sorry Lord.* We exchanged verses of "When I Survey the Wondrous Cross" with our partnering Korean congregation. Angels stood guard as His presence invaded. Isaiah's words of strength and prophesy came to life in a dance between two diverse worlds.

> *"But he was pierced for our transgressions,*
> *he was crushed for our iniquities;*
> *the punishment that brought us peace was upon him,"...*
> *- Isaiah 53:5 (NIV')*

More prayers, then quiet. A period of silence hovered. Then, if I remember correctly, which lately doesn't happen as often as I'd like, the thunderous notes of the piano matched the march of heavens' angels sweeping down the streets of gold - when I shut my eyes.

In the solitude of prayer and melody I heard their voices, *"And He shall reign forever and ever. King of Kings, and Lord of Lords. Hallelujah!"* *Hallelujah Father . . .* Handel's Messiah at Easter, joy and pain. Opening my eyes, I returned to the intimacy of this uncomfortable night.

As the Korean minister opened his mouth, I watched Ian's eyes grow wide. The minister's words, like rapid fire, impressed Ian. *Uh Oh! Here we go; Ian's rendition was ready to burst.* I searched the table for something, *oh, a pen! What are pens doing here?* I pushed the evening program and pen under his nose as fast as I could. *Please God, hold him back from the gibberish that is about to flow.*

Distracted, Ian began to draw as I sighed back into this blessed adventure. Songs and scriptures collided. We broke the Bread of Life and served each other the best we could. Still sitting at the table, nervous laughter arose as we shared communion. Jesus, broken and given to contain all our brokenness. The only One who can complete us - the Host of Heaven, here in this place.

Once again, the quiet invaded. The sounds of spring, birds, crickets in their evensong, filled the darkness now complete. The Garden was calling for the Lonely one. Lights dimmed, candles illuminating, the banquet nearly complete, our journey to the cross began.

As guests of this banquet, we were invited to write down the names of people we were unable to forgive. We could leave all our messes with Christ.

To my left, Danny was busy writing after I spilled out the not so usual suspects on my pink paper. He had stuff only Jesus could heal. My twelve-year-old was writing to Jesus. I could not love away, hug away his hurts. Swallowing my tears, I prayed. *Father, this child is yours. Please take whatever hurts him and whatever stands between You and him. I praise You.*

So that nothing would be between us and His love, there was one more invitation before we dispersed into the night. One by one, each of us brought our sorrows and nailed them onto the barren, vibrant cross. *How they crucified you Lord? How I do so when I don't live in Your will. Forgive me Jesus, again and again and again.* Danny and I waited for each other, each watching the other pound our hurts into the tree of life.

In the van, Ian was noisy and boisterous, again. Ian's response to our unusual quietness was, "Hey, Hey!" I countered, "Wow," in a whisper. Danny offered, "It was all I could do – not to cry. What Jesus did." Nodding as we drove off, the silence interrupted only by Ian's "What? What happened, what are you talking about?" *Oh, autism, you don't have the final say, Jesus is here.*

"And by his wounds we are healed."
- Isaiah 53:5 (NIV')

He never leaves us the same. Amazing? Beautiful? Yes! *Thank you Lord.*

The table is set, a feast prepared,
A Savior offering forgiveness, freedom
Love, Laughter,
More grace and mercy than you'll ever need.
Life - forever with Him
Never fearing the absence of His presence,
a "come as you are" invitation from
the One who loves and waits for you . . .
promises, promises . . .

"For no matter how many promises God has made,
they are "Yes" in Christ. And so through him the "Amen"
is spoken by us to the glory of God."
- 2 Corinthians 1:20 (NIV')

---

[1] *"Handel's Messiah,"* George Frideric Handel, 1685-1759, This work is in the Public Domain.

Believe

Jesus, my strength, my Savior, you are the Lover of my soul.
You are, and that will always be enough to know.
Your Word, spoken thousands of years ago, is still the same;
yesterday, today and tomorrow. Thank you for that promise.

I believe in your Love, I try each day to live your commands
to love even when it's hard, sometimes when it really hurts.
You are our very breath of life. We live in your Love, mercy and
forgiveness, thank You, thank You.

GETTING ON WITH IT
2012-2015

No Room At The . . .

For years, I felt like I was going around the same mountain with the same results. We decided it was vital to re-enroll Ian into our school district. Seeking help one last time in 2012, I no longer looked at these individuals as "the enemy." We didn't know if previous delays and parental/student violations, a.k.a., deliberate attempts not to provide school support, were on the horizon. But this time had to be different. No lawyers, advocates, mediators were invited to this party, only the Living God was the guest of Honor.

"Then Caleb silenced the people before Moses and said,
"We should go up and take possession of the land,
for we can certainly do it."
But the men who had gone up with him said,
"We can't attack those people; they are stronger than we are."
And they spread among the Israelites a bad report about
the land they had explored. They said,
"The land we explored devours those living in it.
All the people we saw there are of great size.
We saw the Nephilim there
(the descendants of Anak come from the Nephilim).
We seemed like grasshoppers in our own eyes,
and we looked the same to them."
- Numbers 13:30-33 (NIV)*

It's funny but when I surrendered Ian's future to God something changed in me. The district staff no longer looked oppressive. They looked human and they acted it all along the way. I felt free to do and pray for what I needed to do with each step. I was strong in the Lord like the scripture encourages. I could stand back and assess progress without becoming emotionally wiped out. That was amazing! *Thank you Lord!!!* Even more stunning was that I could actually pray for them.

"Then Moses and Aaron fell facedown in front
of the whole Israelite assembly gathered there.
Joshua son of Nun and Caleb son of Jephunneh,
who were among those who had explored the land,
tore their clothes and said to the entire Israelite assembly,
"The land we passed through and explored is exceedingly good.
If the LORD is pleased with us, he will lead us into that land,
a land flowing with milk and honey, and will give it to us.
Only do not rebel against the LORD. And do not be afraid
of the people of the land, because we will devour them.

"Their protection is gone, but the LORD is with us.
Do not be afraid of them."
- Numbers 14:5-9 (NIV')

Of course, I pleaded to the One who loves us all. It hurt to hear Ian's aching, "Does He know I need help?" He thought his prayers were not answered because God just did not hear him.

"But if you will seek God earnestly
and plead with the Almighty,
if you are pure and upright,
even now he will rouse himself on your behalf
and restore you to your prosperous state."
- Job 8:5-6 (NIV')

Bud attended every meeting. I did the research, re-learned the law, and prepared our case. I decided, on purpose, to trust God completely, no matter what was going on or what was not working. I made the commitment that He would see us through and believed. Months turned into almost a year and the Lord rescued, nudged, opened my eyes to what needed to be addressed at every turn. Jesus loving each of us was just beautiful.

Many evenings I was wrought with next steps. Like a game of chess, each move had a reaction, sometimes positive, mostly angst. Prepare, pray, be still, Know He is the Lord, Great and Mighty. *Yes, Lord that makes sense.* Going to bed, I would put my concerns to Him, my questions, surrendering to Elohim, Creator God, my Everything. In the morning, the answers unraveled fast, I needed a pen bedside. *Thank you, thank you Lord.*

There were days, I would cry out literally, *I need You desperately.* I cannot get reports. *Ian needs You.* Ian's education meeting coincidentally was planned for the same time Danny was graduating middle school. *I love You. I know You have great plans for Ian and Danny.* Show me what to do. *Please help me make time for Danny.* Addressing the graduates, the new superintendent spoke, ". . . write the vision, make it . . ." *Wait, what?* Did he say what I think he said? Write the vision, make it plain, for Danny's life, Ian's life . . . Old Testament wisdom. A man of God speaking God's Word, making a way for Ian, *Oh Hope of Glory, You still hold us.*

"And the LORD answered me, and said,
Write the vision,
and make it plain upon tables,
that he may run that readeth it."
- Habakkuk 2:2 (KJV)

Be still but keep running, got it! Child Study Team evaluations rolled into Independent Evaluations and the months turned into just about a year, another year without social skills, another year without appropriate support, therapy, education, friends, peers. *Father!* But I knew in my heart to thank Him, to praise Him. Again, I told Him, *I need You desperately.* The Father's, maybe it was the Son's, magnificent return, *"I love you endlessly."* *Thank you Lord.*

All the while, Danny played his trumpet and baritone in school and symphonic concerts, learned the guitar and became quite a skateboarder. An honor student since middle school, he is a kind, sweet young man dedicated to his studies, music and friends. Danny plays the electric guitar in the band, Downstream. So many blessings in one person, he is amazing. *You are so great Lord!*

The process included setbacks caused by discrepancies in reports, incomplete evaluations, Hurricane Sandy and the Case Manager having a family loss. It was twelve years since Ian's first months of pre-school. On December 12, 2012, the school district finally recognized his autism as debilitating and real.

I wondered what was up with all those 12's???? The number twelve must be pretty significant in the eyes of the Creator. I have heard some say it is the number of completion. I love when I can look at scripture and it becomes fresh and new. Scanning **www.BibleGateway.com**, my favorite NIV Bible reference, I found a lot of twelve's:

angels	legions of angels	silver sprinkling
apostles	lions	sons
basketfuls	loaves of bread	springs
baskets	male goats	staffs
bowls	male lambs	stars
brothers	men	stone pillars
crops of fruit	months	stones
cubits	oxen	thrones
days	parts	towns
disciples	patriarchs	tribes
district governors	pearls	years
foundations	pieces	yoke of oxen
gates	rams	young bulls
gold dishes	rulers	
hours	silver plates	
leaders		

We were finally ready to visit schools, thank God! We found a school with a dynamic Social Skills Curriculum and academic opportunities. We were excited about Ian's future. Years before, I had a dream. Ian was in a classroom on the second floor of a school. It was winter and the snow totals were high. Ian was happy and part of a caring school community. I believed God for that vision.

Finding a school that works with students with Asperger's is difficult anywhere, it's more like the square peg round hole syndrome. Ian needed occupational, speech, social and academic support. On one hand, you have out-of-district schools that meet the academic needs of these students but don't address the impact of motor skills, language, or social challenges and vice versus. One school, Newmark Education, wrapped it all together.

We made an appointment to see the school but were told only one slot was open. There were two interviews, one with Ian and another student. Our hearts sank. How could it be? After all these years of struggling, fighting, investigating an appropriate program to meet his needs, we met another obstacle. We found this door open just a crack, and it was ready to close.

Bud urged me to begin a new search. I looked at the websites of the other schools on the list. No, this isn't right I thought to myself as I prayed. Deep calling to deep, I felt His Spirit counsel, "W*ait*."

The nudging went on. I phoned my Mom and broke down crying. How could we come this far, and there is no room for him; did I wait too long? In sixth grade, I had to pull Ian out of school; he was being hit and bullied, injured emotionally and wholly. His spirit was crushed. Homeschooling remediation coupled with Voyagers' Community School a few days a week was then followed by nearly a year of school district home instruction.

During that conversation with my Mom, I pulled myself together and remembered all the times our wonderful Creator rescued us, loved and blessed us. We had been in messes before and everything turned out great. So I believed everything would be alright. Throughout the day and before sleep, I thanked the Lord as I envisioned Ian at Newmark High School, seeing him happy, learning and safe. *Thank you, thank you, thank you Lord.*

> *"She saddled the donkey and said to her servant, "*
> *Lead on; don't slow down for me unless I tell you.*
> *"So she set out and came to the man of God at Mount Carmel.*
> *When he saw her in the distance, the man of God said to his servant Gehazi, "Look!*
> *There's the Shunammite! Run to meet her and ask her, 'Are you all right? Is your*
> *husband all right? Is your child all right?'"*

"Everything is all right," she said."
- 2 Kings 4:24-26 (NIV°)

It didn't look good, but I believed. Part of me was thinking all is well, and the other, am I crazy? For a few weeks in January and the beginning of February, we waited. We were invited to talk after Ian's interview. Newmark made an exception and accepted both students.

Worth the wait, room was made for Ian. He returned to a structured academic program, an environment that his psyche and mind and heart needed. Ian was embraced by Newmark and Grace.

Regardless of abilities, fitting in this world, when you think and act differently, can be difficult. This world however beautiful or chaotic is not our true home. Jesus has made a way being The Way. Jesus comforted his disciples . . .

"Do not let your hearts be troubled. You believe in God;
believe also in me. My Father's house has many rooms;
if that were not so, would I have told you that I am going there
to prepare a place for you? And if I go and prepare a place for you,
I will come back and take you to be with me
that you also may be where I am.
You know the way to the place where I am going."
- John 14:1-4 (NIV°)

How beautiful that a heavenly place awaits those who believe. A place prepared in pain, destined for Love. I think when we make room in our hearts for the King of Glory, remarkably, all are welcome to become His. Here and now, we can choose to live in peace and joy and mercy when we believe.

"And she brought forth her firstborn son,
and wrapped him in swaddling clothes, and laid him in a manger;
because there was no room for them in the inn."
- Luke 2:7 (KJV)

Jesus, gentlemanly enough, waits for us to invite Him in, to create a space where our hearts and His Spirit reside together. There is One for whom there was no room. But for us, that is not the case. As for the winter Ian was accepted into Newmark, we were covered in snow! *Thank you beautiful Light and Love!*

Mrs. Kravitz

Bewitched. I can hear the theme song now. If you were around in the 60's, I'll bet you remember it too. The little twinkle and twitch of Samantha Stephens' nose when her instinct caused her to rely on witchcraft instead of sweating it out like the rest of us humans. Elizabeth Montgomery played a housewife and mom who happened to be a witch. She was clever and pretty. The comedic cast was great with relatives encouraging Samantha to take the easy way out and neighbors who were clueless and nosy. Mrs. Kravitz, Gladys, was always screeching at her husband, Abner, and peeking around Samantha's house and life. Her nosiness got a lot of laughs.

My friend Sally had an email address from another 60's show.[1] When emailing her, I would sign off as Mrs. Kravitz. Yes, I'll admit if something loud happens outside, I check it out. But I do try to stay out of other people's business. A birthday present one year from Sally was the complete first season of Bewitched. When I watched as a kid I wished I could twitch my nose and life would magically become what I imagined. Wouldn't life be a lot simpler if it worked that way? In my "bewitched days" I already *knew* twitching my nose wasn't going to get me anything I happened to want – I already believed in and prayed to this wonderful God.

> *"Not to us, LORD, not to us*
> *but to your name be the glory,*
> *because of your love and faithfulness."*
> *– Psalm 115:1 (NIV*)*

It was the first week of June 2013 and I had five skin biopsies, all on my face. I looked and felt like the walking wounded. It wasn't pretty. If I were Samantha from Bewitched, I would have to manually move my nose instead of wiggling it. By the end of the month I received a phone call that it was basal cell carcinoma, cancer. It was a strange call because it was a technician and not the doctor. They recommended procedures, one being radiation treatments to my nose, before I could even understand what was going on. I could make an appointment with the doctor or schedule a procedure. Whoa!!! I did neither. I asked for my copies of the reports and prayed.

I researched other possible strategies. I learned of an alternative treatment for the same cancer, a cream for non-melanoma skin lesions, and spoke with a person whose cancer was totally removed by it. I prayed again and decided to use this cream instead of a chemotherapy cream that might also kill healthy cells, or surgery which might not get all of the cancer and have to be repeated.

The treatment period was estimated to be three to four months. I began treatment at home, taking pictures of my nose. I snapped my very ugly, oozing selfie at the kitchen sink that first week. Before I took the photo, I asked God to cover me in His love and bless me with healing. It doesn't usually feel like a choice to be so bold.

The word cancer might give anyone chills. I was scared, no longer invincible, gee, was I ever? *Father, am I doing the right thing? The guys need me, I need me. I need You.* I had taken my first selfie a few months earlier for my "Linked In" profile. Tonight's picture would not be a keeper.

There was a fragrance that wasn't there before, ever. A plant given to me years before had a flower ready to bloom. The vines stretched from the sunroom into the kitchen. Its scent was strong. That is so strange I thought to myself. This plant has never flowered.

> *"Flowers appear on the earth;*
> *the season of singing has come,*
> *the cooing of doves*
> *is heard in our land.*
> *The fig tree forms its early fruit;*
> *the blossoming vines spread their fragrance.*
> *Arise, come, my darling;*
> *my beautiful one, come with me."*
> *- Song of Songs 2:12-14 (NIV")*

The blossom was beautiful, bringing me great comfort. I took it as a sign, an answer to my plea moments before that I was going to be okay.

> *"For we are to God the pleasing aroma of Christ*
> *among those who are being saved and those who are perishing.*
> *To the one we are an aroma that brings death;*
> *to the other, an aroma that brings life.*
> *And who is equal to such a task?*
> *Unlike so many, we do not peddle the word of God for profit.*
> *On the contrary, in Christ we speak before God with sincerity,*
> *as those sent from God."*
> *- 2 Corinthians 2:15-17 (NIV")*

It was the start of summer and I could not be in the sun at all. And of course, it was a lovely summer, not too hot, yet spent indoors. The treatment was painful. I was still frightened as the cream penetrated down to the cancer cells burning the skin away leaving me with an open wound. It was gross: no, I was gross.

I continued my daily affirmations of faith and love. The staff from the ointment company emailed often to learn my progress. They were very supportive. *I will give thanks to the Lord for He is good, His mercy endures forever* came out of my mouth repeatedly until the words were in my spirit. Believing in His goodness, my wholeness, His Love gave me courage.

> *"The trumpeters and musicians joined in unison to give*
> *praise and thanks to the Lord.*
> *Accompanied by trumpets, cymbals and other instruments,*
> *the singers raised their voices in praise to the Lord and sang:*
> *"He is good; his love endures forever."*
> *– 2 Chronicles 5:13 (NIV")*

Earlier in the year, we had taken big steps towards holistic living; we began composting, being mindful of our use of paper products, eating organically, collecting and using water from the dehumidifier for indoor and outdoor plants.

When Ian received placement at Newmark, I got back to exercising, joined a yoga class, and started juicing. Filling the quiet in the house, I found The Gary Null Show on Progressive Radio Network, getting hooked on daily nutritional and environmental news. This midday broadcast is filled with healthy ideas and natural alternatives.

I learned that cancer loves sugar so I stopped the treats. I used turmeric and black cumin seed oil for inflammation, and veggies and fruit became staples. I rested when my nose hurt and prayed when uncertainty crept into my spirit.

I also sought out a skin cancer doctor who was willing "to monitor but not treat my condition" as this alternative cream was not in his protocol. He reviewed biopsy results, progress, and offered surgery should the treatment not be successful. The doctor was amazingly kind and thoughtful about my decision.

I never realized the importance of the full use of my nose for sneezing, laughing, or even laying my head on my pillow.

During my oozing days, Sally and I met a few times. Opening a gift she brought to cheer me, I found a beautiful angel pin with a red heart shining from the center. When her children were in elementary school, Sally was diagnosed with breast cancer. She had and has, incredible strength. I didn't know she was going through treatments, I thought she was just fashionably alternating between hip hats. I remember the day we met for coffee, and I gasped to see beautiful new hair growing underneath her wig. It was wonderful to celebrate Sally's joy.

Sally knew how uncomfortable I was, but didn't have to say a word. She shared how others blessed her with angel gifts during her treatment. It lifted her and reminded her that God was with her and loved her. I am not so good with delicate jewelry. A few days later I broke the back of the pin. Then I thought, this angel heart belongs with a necklace I wear daily.

My parents, returning from Italy in 2001, gave me a circular pendant with the PAX Christ sign. It is centered between the Greek symbols for the letters "a" for Alpha and "z" for Omega. It is a unique necklace.

So this beautiful, angel heart resides daily with the symbol of the One who is the Author and Finisher of our very breath. These are beautiful reminders of my parents' love, the Redeemers' promise and an enduring friendship.

> *"He said to me: "It is done.*
> *I am the Alpha and the Omega, the Beginning and the End.*
> *To the thirsty I will give water without cost*
> *from the spring of the water of life."*
> *- Revelation 21:6 (NIV")*

Beginning twice-daily treatments on July 12th, I finished on October 4th. It took two more months for the wound to close. A biopsy couldn't be performed until new growth had covered the gaping wound. Well into winter an in-depth biopsy was undertaken. The doctor shared the cancer was significant, he had to be sure.

Incredibly, a little bud that hung upside on that plant bloomed once again the week I got the biopsy results. When God causes these wonderful sparks of His Love, it gives me goose bumps and makes me wonder what I may have missed along the way.

> *"Then your light will break forth like the dawn,*
> *and your healing will quickly appear; then your*
> *righteousness will go before you, and the glory*
> *of the Lord will be your rear guard."*
> *- Isaiah 58:8 (NIV")*

To my doctor's amazement, no cancer was found, not in the target area or around the wound. It didn't look like a scar but brand new baby skin, whole and complete. A year after the biopsy, this new patch is blending and becoming a part of the rest of my nose, of me. *Father, You are so Good to us, thank you!*

For me, these healings of my heart, mind, body, and soul have been transformative and humbling.

"Therefore, if anyone is in Christ,
the new creation has come:
The old has gone, the new is here!"
- 2 Corinthians 5:17 (NIV°)

Dear Mrs. Kravitz continually put her nose where it didn't belong. As for mine, it was made new. No scar remains. Even better, I am made new each time I surrender to God's Love.

"He who was seated on the throne said,
"I am making everything new!"
Then he said, "Write this down, for these words are
trustworthy and true. Those who are victorious
will inherit all this, and I will be their God
and they will be my children."
- Revelation 21:5,7 (NIV°)

And now I can twitch and wiggle my nose any which way. I asked for, and gratefully received healing – no magic was necessary. Seeking Love Divine, I find the true Healer of Life, again and again. *Thank you Lord.*

Note: In the New International Version of The Holy Bible, *"Jesus heals"* appears 25 times in the New Testament (according to **www.BibleGateway.com**).

[1] My friend is a very sweet and private person. I chose a different name to share her friendship, honoring her privacy.

Papa Can You Hear Me?

Resident Alien. I have often felt like an alien. Yep, right off the spaceship. You've heard it before: I pray, talk to God a lot, thanking, oh yes the occasional begging. *Papa, can you hear me? It's me, I need you, my kids/your kids need you; the world, O Father, the world desperately needs you.*

I don't think I look like SNL's *Church Lady*, at least I hope not. Lord knows my mouth has been compared to that of a truck driver, nor do I call others heathens. Okay, maybe once in a while, but only in jest. I am in this world, but not of this world. Does it show? Seeing the pain of this life, sometimes living it, being resurrected in it too, I know His love and beauty everywhere I look. Do others see it too? I can't be the only one. Where are my fellow aliens?

> *"Beloved, I urge you as aliens and strangers to abstain
> from fleshly lusts which wage war against the soul.
> Keep your behavior excellent
> among the Gentiles, so that in the thing in which
> they slander you as evildoers, they may because of your
> good deeds, as they observe them,
> glorify God in the day of visitation."*
> *- 1 Peter 2:11–12 (NASB)* [1]

It was a warm, sunny Sunday for late September in 2013. Those days are so precious, not quite fall, no longer summer, an in-between time. We were in a new church and learning about the Nicene Creed; why it was needed, what it took to create, what it means for us today, more than just a statement, a living testament. Pastor Jason began with "What we say matters." Almost with the same breath, "It determines how we live and act out our faith."

While the Nicene Creed was scripture for this morning, Pastor's sermon clarified Jerusalem Council's purpose. In 50 A.D. they wrangled with the question of Christ's Divinity.

What I think I heard, I jotted down . . .

We believe one Lord, Jesus Christ, sons and daughters through adoption proceeds from the Father. Examining, dismantling the text and merging it together in Oneness. Of one substance "one in being." Jesus becomes one of us so we can live, follow and understand the language of love.

God's way of communicating to us. *So beautiful is this language of love . . .*

Worshipping together we "hear" God's will in the community of faith. Who is Jesus?

- If Jesus isn't God, we are not forgiven and do not have salvation.
- If Jesus isn't human, we wouldn't have redemption.

We sat and we listened, wrangling with Christ's humanness and His divinity. How could three very separate individuals be of one being, one God? So much information on what felt like an easy breezy Sunday.

As Pastor Jason preached, a young man with intellectual challenges sitting in the front row, chimed in with grunts and groans that only God's Spirit could interpret.

"In the same way, the Spirit helps us in our weakness.
We do not know what we ought to pray for,
but the Spirit himself intercedes for us through wordless groans."
– Romans 8:26 (NIV®)

Pastor moved away from the groans, careful not to go too far, yet distant enough to project his voice. He was careful not to be disrespectful of the young man, but mindful of his congregation.

Almost like a dance of sorts, Pastor with his sermon, the young man with his periodic groans. And yes, the Spirit of Life danced in between them. And me, I prayed Pastor Jason wouldn't be jarred by the inconsistent rhythms of the shout outs.

For just a moment, I was back in time, watching Ian again, snuggled between the kneeler and pew as a youngster. Touch was difficult, finding his body in space a challenge, he crawled, curled himself like a little turtle to find safety and comfort. Growling, grunting, clumsy loudness were part of daily routine on Sunday mornings.

It was not a welcomed routine by churchgoers. He would be on all fours, hands and knees, snarling at my touch with the sign of peace. Growling at those who attempted to shake his hand was the usual. It was not exactly peaceful. We skirted biting at church, barely. Snarky ahead of his time, that guy of mine.

There were some who understood the many faces of autism and whispered a prayer over him, at a comfortable distance. Others squeezed my hand a little longer. Oh but there were others, including kids his age, whose darting eyes held judgment against the growls, fidgeting, non-compliance to the rules of this world, even the Sunday morning ones.

It was in those moments that I wondered how could Jesus hang around their necks if He hadn't made it down about three inches to their hearts? Cutting, judging, yes, on my part. Looks that cut to my core, that questioned, where are their hearts?

My humanness, my pride in the way again. But then, a hug or a wink or the sweet grace in another mom's eye that signaled, "it's alright."

Therapies, prayers, medicine, love, holistic everything, and a whole lot of Jesus moved us along our uncertain journey, leaving Ian upright and strong. At 16, he joined the youth group at Outreach Red Bank (ORB) Church, now called Park Church. Ian enjoyed his first ever weekend away from home on a snowy winter retreat. *Yes, leaving those things that lay behind and pushing ahead . . .*

> *"I press on toward the goal to win the prize for which God*
> *has called me heavenward in Christ Jesus."*
> *- Philippians 3:14 (NIV)*

My attention returned to this service. Grunts ebbed and flowed throughout the sermon. Something inside leapt when I had, perhaps, an alien thought. What if the grunts, here and there, were Jesus shouting out with language all too familiar? *"Hey Jason, doing great, Atta boy!"* Would that be too far out even for this resident alien? His Divineness spilling over into our humanity, *"I love ya guy, keep going!"* A humanity broken yet filled with unending grace, if only they knew. If anyone could hear Jesus' shout outs, would they be too much to bear, to embrace mercy so undeserved?

Did others wonder too, or were they awash in grappling with this Triune God? Thinking to myself, I get you are God, Jesus and Holy Spirit. I accept I may never understand how three in one persons works. And I am good with that, for now.

In a silent prayer, spirit to Spirit, *Papa, thank you for all that you are. Because I am not all that. I praise you and can never repay you for everything; this new day, a new hope, your absolute loveliness, oh I could talk to you all day.*

After reflection time, we sang two bold, beautiful praise songs. The Message had been spoken, sent out, swirling in the very air we breathed.

And so, it was not alien for us to stand, and sing, and sway in celebration of our Lord. Some clap, some dance and sway to an audience of One, singing

"Jesus Messiah" and *"Glorious Day."* The sun was magnificent and the little children sent to Sunday school burst through the door racing and giggling to moms and dads already in the Light of worship. Precious little ones running to be reunited. *Yes, Lord, it's all about you, Jesus, Father, Spirit of Life, mercy, forgiveness, grace, Ancient of Days.*

Two little girls found each other's hands, held on tight, and swayed to the celebration music, back and forth. I watched again, as another little one went running to his father. This time, the Pastor's son hugging, clinging, holding on. Instead of shooing him away to be with Mom, with closing prayer moments away, Pastor Jason reached down, put his arm around his son, and welcomed his youngest into his embrace.

Yes, what we say matters and how we live does too. The Spirit of Love lives and breathes and moves among us each day. In between the groans and grunts of life, He is with us: loving, dancing, embracing, forgiving, welcoming, shouting out, *"Atta girl, Atta boy, I love you, I love you, I love you."*

This resident alien no longer has to ask, *Papa, Abba, Father, my Beginning, End, and in between, can You hear me?* I already know, the answer is yes, yes, yes . . . with joy that is not of this world, I surrender with *thank you, thank you, thank you* . . .

> *"Open my eyes that I may see*
> *wonderful things in your law.*
> *I am a stranger on earth;*
> *do not hide your commands from me.*
> *My soul is consumed with longing*
> *for your laws at all times."*
> *- Psalm 119:18-20 (NIV*)*

---

[1] "Scripture taken from the NEW AMERICAN STANDARD BIBLE ®, Copyright © 1960, 1962, 1963, 1968, 1971, 1972, 1973, 1977, 1995 by The Lockman Foundation. Used by permission."

Celebration

*"Humility is the fear of the Lord;
its wages are riches and honor and life."*
- Proverbs 22:4 (NIV)*

Danny was invited some time ago to play his guitar in the praise band.
It's been great getting to know others in the ever-growing band. What a joy
that he wants to come to service when his body wants to lull him back to
sleep on a Sunday morning. A spirit of Love moves him out of bed and his
sleepiness.

Brian, our former pastor, and Dan, the boys' former youth minister, created
another layer in the foundation of Jesus' love for them. Learning His ways
through sermons, youth activities, and singing contemporary worship songs,
both Ian and Danny prayed to ask Jesus into their hearts. Their lives into
Jesus, well that is a work in progress and a beautiful one. I am grateful to the
One who loves us so.

Ian continues to attend worship at Park Church. He receives unconditional
acceptance and love which never stops amazing me. It's "Ian's place" to
connect with peers and some friends in their twenties. For four years now,
they are lasting friends in Christ. In 2011, Brian took Ian to the youth group
at Park Church. He stayed until Ian felt comfortable to be with the group
himself. Ian got in the groove of informal gatherings, bible readings, worship
services and even spiritual retreats. Relationships grew and Ian's own faith
has too, thank you Dan and Brian!

Danny and I have attended Tower Hill Presbyterian Church for two years
now. Feelings of compassion, welcome, silliness, joy and sometimes tears
erupt as Pastor Jason implores us to unpack the heaviness of our lives. "*Be
still* and know this One true God," he reminds us each Sunday. Simple to say,
not simple to do.

I had my hesitations. The second week we attended, my eyes found a
member of the Child Study Team who withheld student records and stated
Ian didn't need support during his public school years. Her team leader
initiated the children's service investigation against me. *Here Lord, really? I
thought I was done with that wound.*

Just as my adrenalin was settling, at the passing of the peace, I noticed a well-
recognized legislator who did reply to my pleas for Ian during those awful
years. But he didn't know how to help. So he didn't. He assured me the

district offered a program even though it refused to accept Ian's diagnoses and developmental disabilities.

Seeing these two was a jolting reminder of my son's suffering and his brother's immense patience. I begged, A*m I supposed to be here?* I was uncomfortably still. Wish that eighties song from The Clash came to mind then, *"Should I Stay Or Should I Go?"* Maybe then it would have provided some laughter. After composing myself I realized how uncomfortable they must be to see me!

As we began at Tower Hill, Ian was coming up on a year of home instruction after my renewing my efforts with the school district. No student is supposed to be on home instruction that long. It's the most restrictive learning placement. There was no choice but to believe God, to see in my mind's eye, Ian happily settled in a great school, and living a life the years had stolen.

> *". . . And let us run with perseverance the race marked*
> *out for us, fixing our eyes on Jesus,*
> *the pioneer and perfecter of faith.*
> *For the joy set before him he endured the cross,*
> *scorning its shame,*
> *and sat down at the right hand of the throne of God.*
> *Consider him who endured such opposition from sinners,*
> *so that you will not grow weary and lose heart."*
> *- Hebrews 12:1-3 (NIV*)*

Spirit of Life, how you Love.

> *"Therefore, strengthen your feeble arms and weak knees.*
> *"Make level paths for your feet,"*
> *so that the lame may not be disabled,*
> *but rather healed."*
> *- Hebrews 12:12-13 (NIV*)*

At first, I didn't tell Danny about "the two," who they were or what their roles could have meant for Ian's life. Still in The Clash zone, I shared with my friend Tammy: "What if they ask how Ian is?" (Danny and I lived watching the paralyzing anxiety, loneliness, isolation, the obsessive behaviors, the pulling at his hair, eyebrows, hands.) "What do I tell them?" Without hesitation came Tammy's unwavering response: "You say Ian is getting stronger and stronger every day." Wow, that works, empowering yes, and so there! Thank you Tammy!

Reflecting on Celebration, that's the name of our worship service, brings great comfort. Celebration continues to grow, I mean really grow. Ushers are busy adding chairs as the service begins well into the passing of peace. Many talented musicians, including Danny, participate in the praise band, giving all of us a new chance to give thanks, sing praise, cherish our God. *How we need You Lord.*

To see His young one, Danny my treasure, who gave his heart to Jesus some time ago, rocking his guitar, wrapped in headphones and Love, what more could a mom ask for? But of course I do. I pray for the understanding of God for both guys' minds and hearts. If we have His heart, if we live for Him, if we learn His ways and live them, isn't that cause for celebration, every day?

As of today in 2015, no meaningful words have been exchanged with the two who so concerned me. A smile here and there, passing peace with one, giving my offering to the other, Forgiveness leads the way. Between us only the Sacred speaks. Be still.

> *"For if you forgive other people when they sin against you,*
> *your heavenly Father will also forgive you.*
> *But if you do not forgive others their sins,*
> *your Father will not forgive your sins."*
> *- Matthew 6:14-15 (NIV®)*

At Tower Hill, little girls sway their clasped hands together, a deaf mom is joyous as her son beats on the jumbie (a really cool steel drum), grandmothers wipe away tears with blessed assurance, a father bows his head, a young mom takes a baptismal plunge, and an Iraq veteran's mom lives out her thankfulness in service. Each week there is more.

We celebrate our Father's Love, our Savior's sacrifice and the Spirit Divine, Who makes room for all humanity to dwell within *His* absolute Divinity. O Praise Him you angels, the peoples of the earth. The King of Glory we celebrate: the Cornerstone of Life we honor. Oh weary world, He makes us new each day, when we let Him.

> *"Let the message of Christ dwell among you richly*
> *as you teach and admonish one another with all wisdom*
> *through psalms, hymns, and songs from the Spirit,*
> *singing to God with gratitude in your hearts."*
> *- Colossians 3:16 (NIV®)*

On beautiful spring days, on snow-filled days, on hot beach days, on crisp fall days, when our lives are filled, when our hearts are empty, when there is no peace to be found, there is a celebration . . .

to give honor,
a time to praise,
a time to give,
a time for tears,
a time to bless,
a time to pause,
a time for laughter,
a time to forgive,
a time to offer peace,
a time to worship,
a time to pray,
a time to dance,
a time to surrender.

May it delight the True Keeper of Time, the Breath of Life, the Triumphant One, giving glory to *The Word from the Beginning*. Be still indeed!

*"Therefore, since we are receiving a kingdom
that cannot be shaken, let us be
thankful, and so worship God acceptably
with reverence and awe,
for our God is a consuming fire."
– Hebrews 12:28-29 (NIV*)*

High Anxiety

Danny drove to his Monday guitar lesson less than a week after he passed his driving test. He got his license the morning of another snowstorm. The winter of 2015 had been brutal, with snow and ice everywhere. The roads he would take were familiar, but he would see them differently as a driver. I could have paced the house, pretended to make dinner, or prayed. I started praying before he backed out of the driveway.

I blessed him on his way. I do that whenever the guys and I leave each other. Danny is a safe driver. It was dusk and the first time he was driving by himself. I believe in God's Love for Danny. I kept myself busy instead of thinking. The Lord's Prayer swirled around my head and being. *Thank you Lord for cell phones and the "k" that lit my screen on his arrival!*

> *"Yes, my soul, find rest in God;*
> *my hope comes from him."*
> *– Psalm 62:5 (NIV")*

Thinking. I know, I think too much. But I am trying to give it up, well not completely. When the guys were in grade school, I was fortunate to have a sitter for a little while. She would give me a chance to run errands without dragging them along. The days were filled with keeping up with what was or was not going on in Ian's classroom. The afternoons were stacked with medical and therapy appointments. An occasional chance to get out helped quiet my mind. Our sitter would have a ton of homework as an honor student. From time to time, it overwhelmed her. When she arrived, I welcomed her to "Anxiety Central," which hopefully made her feel at home. Here, no worry was too little. We had 'em all and then some, that is until I read and studied God's Word.

My former brain gym instructor's mantra was "Energy follows intention." Where was I putting my energy? Falling short some days, I intended to fix my eyes on Jesus and move through my days. And that included understanding what the stories of the bible meant for Ian, Danny and myself. What was God teaching me each day? What was the lesson I needed to learn?

God's personal Love for us was right there in scripture! I could let go of my control of everything and believe in this Perfect Love. *Thank you Father!*

> *"There is no fear in love; but perfect love casts out fear,*
> *because fear involves torment.*
> *But he who fears has not been made perfect in love."*
> *- 1 John 4:18 (NKJV)*

I have told the guys there are plenty of times in my life I am afraid. But being afraid doesn't mean you stand still until the fear has passed. I have and continue to walk through the rooms of our home saying, "No fear here. You don't belong here. God is here, and I am well able. I am a child of the Most High God." *Thank you Jesus You are here!*

> *"So if the Son sets you free, you will be free indeed."*
> *- John 8:36 (NIV®)*

Mel Brooks' movies *"High Anxiety"* and *"Young Frankenstein"* are favorites in our home. We know a thing or two about fear *and* being "abby normal." Gratefully, laughter has been some of the best medicine in our lives. When it's not enough, remembering God's past compassion stirs me with His Light and Love. The more I thanked Him, the more new discoveries of healing manifested all around us. It is beautiful, like Him. *Thank you Lord.*

> *"Our mouths were filled with laughter,*
> *our tongues with songs of joy.*
> *Then it was said among the nations,*
> *"The LORD has done great things for them."*
> *- Psalm 126:2 (NIV®)*

There is something ironic about Mel Brooks' sense of humor. The song from the movie is catchy and funny but the anxiety his character portrayed in *"High Anxiety"* was overwhelming. Living with anxiety is a painful reminder of our human frailty. Having been stuck myself on thoughts that go round and round in my mind has not been life affirming. Paralyzing anxiety has impacted Ian over the years. This anxiety has been debilitating and makes everything in our world stop.

Ian's reaction to prescriptions for anxiety did just the opposite. They increased his anxiety and negative emotions. We know that medicine isn't enough. There is One whose Grace is sufficient to prompt us to seek and find holistic, loving ways to dispel this awful darkness.

> *"But he said to me, "My grace is sufficient for you,*
> *for my power is made perfect in weakness."*
> *Therefore I will boast all the more gladly about my weaknesses,*
> *so that Christ's power may rest on me."*
> *- 2 Corinthians 12:9 (NIV®)*

According to **www.BibleGateway.com**, the word "distress" is mentioned over 100 times in the Old and New Testaments. Our Comforter is with us in our distress. During those times of uncertainty (sleepless nights, educational battles, illnesses, daily vomiting episodes, emotional meltdowns) I held onto this scripture, these empowering Words of Love. I chose to believe in our Lord's reminder of how He equipped us with power. It is more comfortable sometimes to dwell on what we cannot do instead of what we might accomplish. So out of my comfort zone, I repeated out loud and often, these words of St. Paul:

"For God hath not given us the spirit of fear;
but of power, and of love, and of a sound mind."
- 2 Timothy 1:6 (KJV)

The more I spoke of who we are in Christ, the more answers were revealed. In 2013, we learned that Ian and I have the double gene of MTHFR, a gene mutation found in the 2001 Human Genome Project. MTHFR is an enzyme in our bodies that is related to cardiovascular and many neurological diseases. For us it is related to anxiety, autism and Obsessive-Compulsive Disorder (OCD).[1]

We began a protocol of adding Methylated b vitamins into our daily supplementation. People who have this mutation cannot absorb b vitamins through the blood-brain barrier. The transformation of clarity for Ian and not thinking everything to death for me was amazing. Many medical professionals are unaware of the MTHFR enzyme deficiency and its role in living life with vitality.

"So Abraham called that place The LORD Will Provide.
And to this day it is said, "On the mountain of the LORD it will be provided."
- Genesis 22:14 (NIV")

In Ian's newfound clarity, he announced to his father and me that he was not going to return to Newmark. "I am not the same, I am not who I used to be," he pleaded. He wasn't, and neither was I. But we knew Newmark was a place of nurturing and meaningful education. Ian acknowledged he used to be like the other kids, making noises, acting inappropriately, but he wasn't like that anymore. He had changed.

It was spring 2014. School was not over and the principal had phoned about summer plans. Admittedly, everyone at school noticed Ian's progress. During the conversation I was told, "You know Mrs. Baker, Ian is going to have anxiety all his life. He is going to have to accept that reality." Oh boy I thought, I don't accept that reality! Everything is subject to change.

> *"So they brought him. When the spirit saw Jesus,*
> *it immediately threw the boy into a convulsion.*
> *He fell to the ground and rolled around, foaming at the*
> *mouth. Jesus asked the boy's father, "How long has he been*
> *like this?" "From childhood," he answered. "It has often*
> *thrown him into fire or water to kill him. But if you can do*
> *anything, take pity on us and help us."*
> *"'If you can'?" said Jesus.*
> *"Everything is possible for one who believes."*
> *- Mark 9:20-23 (NIV®)*

My summer spent indoors from the sun because of skin cancer was also filled with months of research about the MTHFR and seeking support. Ian, starting Newmark four months before summer break, managed to return to Newmark in the fall. I learned about nutritional, enzyme and mineral deficiencies. Organic foods and exercise were key to improving wellness. His edginess and reminders of how different he'd become only increased. It would take another year and half to find a doctor who understood the MTHFR. We made changes little by little in between.

In 2007, my precious Uncle Victor gave me an enlightening book, "The Power of Your Subconscious Mind" by Dr. Joseph Murphy. With Uncle Victor's guidance and love, the boys and I have used the affirmations found in the book for love, health, focus, harmony and forgiveness. We end each one with "through Jesus Christ!"

Uncle Victor shared: "See Ian well, healed, positive, happy in your mind. You must visualize him at peace. Think that he is all these things, now!" And so, Ian continued his meltdowns, stomped away as emotion swept over him, vomited when stress was heightened and was physically paralyzed with anxiety in his day-to-day life.

> *"For this reason I remind you to fan into flame the gift of God,*
> *which is in you through the laying on of my hands."*
> *- 2 Timothy 1:6 (NIV®)*

Defying every spirit and hindrance to Ian's well being, I stood with the armor of God's Word in the kitchen, in his bedroom, all throughout the house. I announced "Ian is healed, blessed and prosperous. He can do all things through Christ who strengthens him." I spoke into the dry bones of Ian's life and grasped the promises of my Savior. At night, during the twilight before I settled into sleep, I closed my eyes and saw Ian coming through the door after school, happy, telling me what a great day he had. I set the vision in my heart and made it simple.

> *"The hand of the LORD was on me,*
> *and he brought me out by the Spirit of the LORD*
> *and set me in the middle of a valley; it was full of bones.*
> *He led me back and forth among them,*
> *and I saw a great many bones on the floor of the valley,*
> *bones that were very dry. He asked me,*
> *"Son of man, can these bones live?"*
> *I said, "Sovereign LORD, you alone know."*
> *Then he said to me, "Prophesy to these bones and say to them,*
> *'Dry bones, hear the word of the LORD!*
> *This is what the Sovereign LORD says to these bones:*
> *I will make breath enter you, and you will come to life.*
> *I will attach tendons to you and make flesh come upon*
> *you and cover you with skin; I will put breath in you,*
> *and you will come to life.*
> *Then you will know that I am the LORD.'"*
> *- Ezekiel 37:1-6 (NIV®)*

By the end of sophomore year, Ian made his own declarations amidst lingering anxiety. Academics were not working towards his benefit. As we uncovered more of the situation, I took Ian to the Reverend Karen Herrick, PhD, a life coach and spiritual psychologist. With Karen, Ian voiced his desire to have a typical high school experience. Ian's work with Karen revealed his need to decide his future. He discovered his voice which set change in motion. In four short months, working with a caring Case Manager, we found a school to match Ian's present abilities and goals. School delays were history!!! *Thank you Lord!*

I didn't know that Ian's stance would fulfill a dream I had well over a year before.

Part of the dream included Ian, Danny and Bud walking in a park with leaves scattered all over the ground. I saw Ian standing next to Danny. His spirit was that of Danny's, kind and sweet. Leading them was a good shepherd. Upon waking, I was refreshed and so peaceful. My heart was grateful to see Ian happy. I made no connection to Jesus at the time but later laughed out loud when I learned who owned the property of Collier High School, Ian's new school. It was the Sisters of the Good Shepherd.

Somewhere in my heart, in God's countenance, we knew change was necessary. Ian's declaration was not a surprise but a confirmation of his growth. Our lives, Ian's being, become sweeter, more beautiful and peaceful with each day.

With the combination of these supports we have witnessed wonderful improvements. I kept a journal of progress:

- Reduced OCD behaviors, outbursts, meltdowns, frustration, self-talk, panic attacks, and nightmares
- More restful sleep, laughter, happiness and consideration of others
- Increased ability to: tolerate changes in sensory stimuli and routine, apologize when appropriate, plan and make healthier nutritional choices

These are welcome signs of healing. *How you love Ian, Lord!*

The transformation was not overnight. The three of us will never be the same; we evolve, day by day, into His Love. We perceive Ian's new reality right now: attending prom, participating in the school play, acting in a music video, and moving from glory to glory. And we give our Breath of Life all the glory! *Thank you Jesus!!!*

> *"Jesus replied, "Very truly I tell you,*
> *no one can see the kingdom of God*
> *unless they are born again."*
> *- John 3:3 (NIV*)*

I have seen the goodness of the Lord in the land of the living and am so grateful. *Spirit of Life I praise You!*

> *"For you, LORD, have*
> *delivered me from death,*
> *my eyes from tears,*
> *my feet from stumbling,*
> *that I may walk before the LORD*
> *in the land of the living."*
> *- Psalm 116:8-9 (NIV*)*

Note: More about the MTHFR gene and the Rev. Karen Herrick, PhD can be found in Recommended Resources on p. 134.

[1] Obsessive-Compulsive Disorder, OCD is an anxiety disorder and is characterized by recurrent, unwanted thoughts (obsessions) and/or repetitive behaviors (compulsions). Source: **www.nimh.nih.gov.**

It Is Well

I suppose one of the most emotional difficulties of living our new kind of normal, just the three of us, was how others judged us. "*You should, you should have,*" easily flowed from well and not so well-intentioned mouths. And it hurt. Like a river flowing, opinions and judgment were plenty, and they held me prisoner. As the years have rolled along, I realized I had let them.

> *"There is a river whose streams make glad the city of God,*
> *the holy place where the Most High dwells.*
> *God is within her, she will not fall;*
> *God will help her at break of day.*
> *Nations are in uproar, kingdoms fall;*
> *he lifts his voice, the earth melts."*
> *- Psalm 46:4-6 (NIV*)*

In the process of being made over, molded, shaped, pruned, (oh I didn't like the pruning), I became aware of the sweetness of Divine Love. I chose to fix my heart on Jesus alone, the lover of my less than perfect soul, rather than accept the criticism. It would always exist in one form or another. In my surrender to the Giver of Life, it became freeing to release the past and embrace the present. Trading in the *what are you gonna do,* to living in the now, didn't come naturally. But supernaturally, God has shown the boys and me, time and again, in our sweet yet complicated life, all things are possible with Him. *Thank you Abba!*

> *"Set your minds on things above,*
> *not earthly things."*
> *- Colossians 3:2 (NIV*)*

Similar to Frank Sinatra's description of who he was in the song *"That's Life,"* I've been a lot of things too, but in a different order. Raised Roman Catholic, I have worshipped as a Pentecostal, Episcopalian, Lutheran, Baptist, and currently, as a Presbyterian. What all these denominations gratefully have in common is the tenet that Jesus Christ **is** the Son of God, the Savior of all. When my Mom asks, "What are you?" I tell her, "I am a follower of Jesus." I have witnessed worship in many forms. But I didn't find "faith" in a physical building. It was found in surrendering my life to Jesus. *Amen Lord.*

> *"Consequently, faith comes from hearing*
> *the message, and the message is heard*
> *through the word about Christ."*
> *- Romans 10:17 (NIV*)*

One word that I have heard preached with rarity and tenderness is Agape Love. If I understand it correctly, it is the highest form of Love, a love selflessly radiating from the Creator to mankind, His creations. I can't help but smile when I open the refrigerator door each day reaching for a supplement with the same name. While I take these vitamins to help with my own healing process, it is a lovely daily reminder about God's presence in all things. It is more astounding that in my longing to know Him more, He leads me to new sacred scriptures expressing this Love for us all. *Thank you Spirit Divine!*

> *"For now we see only a reflection as in a mirror;*
> *then we shall see face to face.*
> *Now I know in part; then I shall know fully,*
> *even as I am fully known.*
> *And now these three remain:*
> *faith, hope and love.*
> *But the greatest of these is love."*
> *- 1 Corinthians 13:12-13 (NIV*)*

Wherever we attended church, one song always shook me to my core. I am pretty sure I consistently choked out the hymn *"It Is Well With My Soul."* Could anything be well with my soul?

> *"Now faith is confidence in what we hope for*
> *and assurance about what we do not see.*
> *This is what the ancients were commended for.*
> *By faith we understand that the universe was formed at God's command,*
> *so that what is seen was not made out of what was visible."*
> *- Hebrews 11:1-3 (NIV*)*

During the early years after Bud, one thing was consistent beside prayers each day: our bedtime ginger ale toasts. Gathering at the kitchen counter, we filled punch glasses and toasted to the day that had passed, and to the one that would begin as we slept. Clicking our glasses one by one, then together, it was a time to be together and know in that moment that all was well in our world.

> *"Truly he is my rock and my salvation;*
> *he is my fortress, I will not be shaken."*
> *- Psalm 62:6 (NIV*)*

What I couldn't see off in the future were the kind apologies from people in our lives: a former neighbor, a school staff member and a church member. Each expressed sorrow for not understanding the circumstances of our lives. Some asked forgiveness for not doing more, for not realizing what we were going through. Their apologies, never anticipated, filled me with His Grace. What a God, to bring past offenses full circle. Letting go of the past, forgiving and praying for those no longer in my life is possible. My spirit releases them and I give them to God. It is absolutely freeing! That's the way our Savior loves. *Thank you Love's Way!*

"Thomas said to him,
"Lord, we don't know where you are going,
so how can we know the way?"
Jesus answered, "I am the way and the truth and the life.
No one comes to the Father except through me.
If you really know me, you will know my Father as well.
From now on, you do know him and have seen him."
- John 14:5-7 (NIV")

When strife comes, and it does, sometimes relentlessly, with thanks and praise I kneel before The Throne of Grace. Through faith, prayer and meditation, I am continuously received and rescued. I was broken into new by the One who rules the world from heaven's Mercy Seat. That's Love in the making, or perhaps it is the making of faith.

Yes, Father God, Yes, Jesus the Christ, Yes, Holy Spirit, it is well with my soul! Hallelujah!

Faith

"Have faith in God," Jesus answered.

"Truly I tell you, if anyone says to this mountain,
'Go, throw yourself into the sea,'
and does not doubt in their heart but believes
that what they say will happen, it will be done for them.

Therefore I tell you, whatever you ask for in prayer,
believe that you have received it, and it will be yours."
- Mark 11:22-24 (NIV®)

ABOUT THE AUTHOR

Victoria Baker is a writer, photographer, single parent of two sons, and creator of three websites. For nearly 15 years, Victoria has advocated for programs and therapeutic services on behalf of her older son with Asperger's Syndrome, a form of autism.

In addition to testifying before the New Jersey Senate Education Committee, advocacy included several state education mediations and insurance appeals. Victoria developed and taught a special education home school program which led to consulting and writing for **Time4Learning.com**.

Her websites offer resources and encouragement to people living with or loving people with special needs. After a diagnosis of celiac disease, Victoria's experiences have also helped those seeking holistic lifestyle choices including organic and gluten-free living. Victoria's love of trees, in all seasons, are a focus of her photography.

Recommended Resources and a list of Therapies for Special Needs can be found on pages 134 and 135.

Information from both www.sharingsacredspaces.com and www.imoveforlifechannel.com will soon be available at www.victoriabaker.net.

Please visit **www.victoriabaker.net**!

SPECIAL THANKS

With special thanks to *Ian* and *Danny* whose courage and kindness
are daily inspirations. You are my treasures
and I will always love you for you.

****

To *Sarah Lawser*, my dear Editor,
thank you for your generous time
and spirit. I am forever grateful for your
wisdom, and most especially your friendship
and love. Thank you for everything!

****

To my very first reader reviewers: Jill, Carol, Susan, & Catherine

Thank you for your honesty and feedback. You are each beautiful in your
own unique way. I thank God for you each day. Thank you for bringing your
love and wisdom to "The Making of Faith." Giving glory to God is how each
of you live life. I am grateful for your constant examples that shape my life.

****

Mom & Dad, I am forever grateful for you both.

"The Universe is Yours, Be Gentle With It."
- Divine Holy Spirit speaking to my spirit a lifetime ago,
when sweet toddlers were napping.

ACKNOWLEDGEMENTS

I extend special thanks to the following for their kind permissions support. Credit lines are found on pages where works are quoted. I hope including portions of these special works will enhance your reading of "The Making of Faith."

Thank you for making a difference in our lives . . .

The Holy Bible
New American Standard Bible
New Century Version
New Int'l Version
The King James Version
The New King James Version

Brian A. Wren
David Haas
E.E. Cummings
George James Firmage
George Frideric Handel
Marty Haugen
Maurice Bell
Max Lucado
MercyMe
Reuben Morgan
Robert Lowry
Susan Briehl

Bible Gateway
Biblica, Inc.
GIA Publications, Inc.
Harper Collins Christian Publishing
Hillsong United
Hope Publishing Company
Liveright Publishing Corporation
Lockman Foundation
Merriam-Webster's Collegiate ®
Dictionary, Eleventh Edition © 2014
Library of Congress
Microsoft Encarta
Oregon Catholic Press
The Trust of e.e. cummings
Thomas Nelson Publishers
W. W. Norton & Company
Zondervan

Collier High School
Newmark Education
Voyagers' Community School

THE HOLY BIBLE
TRANSLATION ACKNOWLEDGEMENTS

With great thanks for all these works that have showed God's Love alive in these sacred texts and in our ordinary lives. Thank you!

New American Standard
Scripture taken from the NEW AMERICAN STANDARD BIBLE ®, Copyright © 1960, 1962, 1963, 1968, 1971, 1972, 1973, 1977, 1995 by The Lockman Foundation. Used by permission.

New Century Version
Scripture taken from the New Century Version®. Copyright © 2005 by Thomas Nelson, Inc. Used by permission. All rights reserved.

New International Version
Scripture quotations marked (NIV) are taken from the Holy Bible, New International Version®, NIV®. Copyright © 1973, 1978, 1984, 2011 by Biblica, Inc.™ Used by permission of Zondervan. All rights reserved worldwide. **www.zondervan.com** The "NIV" and "New International Version" are trademarks registered in the United States Patent and Trademark Office by Biblica, Inc.™

The King James Version (Public Domain in the United States)

The New King James Version
Scripture taken from the New King James Version ®. Copyright © 1982 by Thomas Nelson. Used by permission. All rights reserved.

ALPHABETICAL PASSAGE ORDER

WHAT READERS HAVE SAID

He Loves Us So

"OH MY, A BLESSING ON YOUR HEAD!
This was extraordinary, and I cried . . ."
Lenore B.

"Short, sweet, and
with a powerful message." Lydia S.

". . . keep fighting the good fight." Renee S.

Bowing Daffodils

"I will never look at a daffodil
the same way again." Sarah L.

The Table Was Set

"It reveals your authenticity and
transparency before the Lord in the
midst of the real suffering of your
experience." Brother Jude L.

". . . with moments in the story that
are humorous, poignant, quirky,
tense, & serene." Larry S.

"I took away from the story the need
to find peace and forgiveness within
myself." Susan S.

Thank you friends for your earliest reading
of particular passages before
"The Making of Faith" was woven together.
Please consider sharing your thoughts at

www.victoriabaker.net

RECOMMENDED RESOURCES

Organizations

Brain Gym, Int'l; **www.braingym.org**
Dianne Craft; Child Diagnostics; **www.diannecraft.org**
Family Resource Associates; **www.frainc.org**
Fearless Parent; **www.fearlessparent.org**
Home School Legal Defense Association; **www.hslda.org**
Karen Herrick; **www.karenherrick.com**
Oasis tlc, 'because children with autism grow up'; **www.oasistlc.org/#!**
Pocketful of Therapy; **www.pfot.com**
Progressive Radio Network with Gary Null, PhD; **www.prn.com**
Switch On Your Brain, Caroline Leaf, PhD; **www.dr.leaf.com**
The ARC; **www.thearc.org**
Wrightslaw Special Education & Advocacy; **www.wrightslaw.com**
www.drnorthrup.com/watch-listen/radio/
www.mthfr.net; **www.methyl-life.com**/symptoms-of-mthfr.html

Books

Brain Integration Therapy Manual, Dianne Craft, MA, CNHP
Creative Visualization, Shakti Gawain
Jesus Calling, Sarah Young
Magnificent Mind at any Age, Daniel Amen, M.D.
Right Brain Phonics Program, Dianne Craft, MA CNHP
Smart Moves: Why Learning is Not all in Your Head, Carla Hannaford,
Tapping The Source, Gladstone, Greninger, Selby
The Blessing, John Trent, PhD & Dr. Gary Smalley
The Power of Awareness, Neville Goddard
The Power of Your Subconscious Mind, Dr. Joseph Murphy
Vaccine Epidemic, Louise Kuo Habakus, M.A. & Mary Holland, J.D.
Who Switched Off My Brain?, Caroline Leaf, PhD
Women's Bodies, Women's Wisdom, Christiane Northrup, M.D.
You Can Heal Your Life, Louise Hay
You're Not Finished Yet, Rev. Karen Herrick, PhD, LCSW, LMSW,
CADC

Documentaries

Autism Made in the USA, Gary Null
Bought, Jeff Hays
Seeds of Death, Gary Null

THERAPIES FOR SPECIAL NEEDS

These private therapies helped Ian, and his gusto for not giving up which made a difference each day. You are so brave Ian, and Danny, you are amazingly compassionate. Thank you my treasures!

Acupressure, Self-Administered
Audio, Visual, Writing Re-Patterning
Brain Gym Int'l Exercises
Brain Integrative Therapy
Brainware, Empowered Learning
Brushing & Joint Compressions
Cognitive Behavioral Therapy
Earobics
Family Psychology & Counseling
Food Therapy
Heart Focus
Holistic Lifestyle
Homeopathy
Interactive Metronome
Kinesiology
Language Therapy
Life Affirmations
MTHFR nutritional supports
Neuro-Feedback
Occupational Therapy with therapist and
for home
Organic Juicing Nutrition
Physical & Aquatic Therapies
Right Brain Phonics Program
Sensory/Motor Therapy
Sibling Therapy
Social Skills Therapy
Visual Therapy

A LETTER TO READERS

Dear Friend,

"The Making of Faith" is a deeply personal exposé of Love in action. It is filled with bold prayers and desperate petitions. Use these prayers freely with my love. Maybe it can help you renew your relationship, create your own meditative practice or intimate conversations with our Redeemer.

I pray you will be able to return to any story in "The Making of Faith" and feel closer to God. May they remind you that no matter what you are facing in life, He is with you and loves you. With God, all things are subject to change.

It has meant a lot to me that you have read "The Making of Faith." The poem on the following page is my thanks to you for being here.

This unimaginable God loves each of us, endlessly, with every breath we breathe.

Peace & Blessings,

Victoria

P.S. You may wonder what happened in 2011 where there was no story recorded. It was a time of homeschooling, driving three days a week to Voyagers', and a beautiful time with the boys. During my drives, I stopped to take pictures of the nature around us. What's next? Perhaps a book of beauty unfolding. We'll see!

A POEM FOR YOU

i thank You God for most this amazing

i thank You God for most this amazing
day: for the leaping greenly spirits of trees
and a blue true dream of sky; and for everything
which is natural which is infinite which is yes

(i who have died am alive again today,
and this is the sun's birthday; this is the birth
day of life and of love and wings: and of the gay
great happening illimitably earth)

how should tasting touching hearing seeing
breathing any-lifted from the no
of all nothing-human merely being
doubt unimaginable You?

(now the ears of my ears awake and
now the eyes of my eyes are opened) [1]
e.e. cummings

27923434R00089

Made in the USA
Middletown, DE
26 December 2015